THE ETHICS OF MANAGEMENT

The Irwin Series in Management and The Behavioral Sciences

Consulting Editors:

L. L. Cummings
Northwestern University

E. Kirby Warren
Columbia University

The Ethics of Management

LARUE TONE HOSMER
Graduate School of Business Administration
University of Michigan

1987

Homewood, Illinois 60430

ISBN 0-256-03480-X

Library of Congress Catalog Card No. 86–81804

Printed in the United States of America

1 2 3 4 5 6 7 8 9 0 F 4 3 2 1 0 9 8 7

Preface

What is "right" and "proper" and "just"? These terms, and that question, are going to become more important in the future than in the past as our society becomes more crowded, our economy more competitive, and our technology more complex. These terms and that question are going to become particularly important for the business executive, whose decisions can affect so many people in ways that are outside their own control.

The ethics of management—the determination of what is "right" and "proper" and "just" in the decisions and actions that affect other people—goes far beyond simple questions of bribery, theft, and collusion. It focuses on what our relationships are—and ought to be—with our employees, our customers, our stockholders, our creditors, our suppliers, our distributors, and our neighbors—members of the communities in which we operate. What do we owe to an employee who has been with the company for twenty-eight years, yet now is no longer needed? What do we owe to a customer who purchased one of our mechanical products three years ago when we now realize that it may fail in operation and cause that person great inconvenience and perhaps some loss of safety? What do we owe to a distributor who helped us establish a major product line years ago, yet now represents an inefficient means of reaching the market? What do we owe to our stockholders, and how do we balance our duties to our stockholders with our obligations to these other groups?

This is the most critical issue in the ethics of management: the continual conflict between the economic performance of the firm, measured by revenues, costs, and profits and owed to the stockholders, and the social performance of the firm, much more difficult to measure but represented by obligations to employees, customers, creditors, suppliers, distributors, and members of the general public. If we discharge our employee who has twenty-eight years of service but is no longer needed, our costs will go down, yet his life may be ruined. If we don't tell our customer about the design flaw in our product our warranty expenses will be lower, yet she may be seriously inconvenienced and perhaps even hurt. If we replace our distributor by shipping directly from the factory to the retailers, our profits will increase, yet we may force that company out of business.

How do we decide when we face such issues? How do we determine what is "right" and "proper" and "just" in these and other instances?

This book looks at how we decide. It first considers the nature of the ethical dilemma in business—this conflict between economic and social performance. Ethical dilemmas in management are not simple choices between "right" and "wrong"; they are complex judgments on the balance between economic returns and social damages, complicated by the multiple alternatives, extended consequences, uncertain probabilities, and career implications that are an inherent part of these decisions.

The book then examines three alternative means of arriving at a decision when faced with an ethical conflict:

1. Economic analysis, relying on impersonal market forces.
2. Legal analysis, relying on impersonal social forces.
3. Ethical analysis, relying on personal moral values.

None of these means of analysis is satisfactory by itself. But all together the analyses do form a means of moral reasoning that can help a manager arrive at a decision that he or she can feel to be "right" and "proper" and "just." The book makes no effort to dictate what is "right" and "proper" and "just"; instead, that is left to the individual's own moral standards of behavior and ethical systems of belief. The intent is to help individuals understand their own moral standards and ethical norms, beliefs, and values so that they can decide when faced with a business dilemma.

Last, let me say that I am not the only person to have thought about the question of what is "right" and "proper" and "just" in management. There are many others—theorists and practitioners. I have learned greatly from both groups and should like to acknowledge my debt to Richard DeGeorge (Kansas), Manuel Velasquez (Santa Clara), Thomas Donaldson (Loyola of Chicago), Patricia Werhane (Loyola of Chicago), Kenneth Goodpasture (Harvard), Gerald Cavanagh (Detroit), William Frederick (Pittsburgh), Edwin Epstein (Berkeley), Oliver Williams (Notre Dame), Lisa Newton (Fairfield), and Kirk Hanson (Stanford). I thank you all.

LaRue Tone Hosmer

Contents

3   Managerial Ethics and the Rule of Law   62

Law as a Guide to Moral Choice. An Example of Moral Choice.
Law as Combined Moral Judgments. Definition of the Law:
Consistent. Universal. Published. Accepted. Enforced. Relationships
between the Law and Moral Standards. Formation of the Law:
Individual Processes. Formation of the Law: Group Processes.
Formation of the Law: Social Processes. Formation of the Law:
Political Process. Conclusions in the Rule of Law as the Basis for
Moral Choice.

4   Managerial Ethics and Normative Philosophy   90

Definition of Normative Philosophy. Ethical Relativism. Eternal
Law. Utilitarianism: A Teleological Theory. Universalism: A
Deontological Theory. Distributive Justice. Personal Liberty.
Conclusions on Normative Philosophy as the Basis for Moral
Choice.

5   Managerial Ethics and Individual Decisions   123

Ethical Analysis and the Lockheed Bribery Case. Ethical Analysis
and a Justifiable Bribery Case. Ethical Analysis and Ethical
Dilemmas: *Pricing of Checking Account Services. Exaggerated or
Misleading Claims in Advertising. Misuse of "Frequent Flyer" Discounts
and Trips. Working Conditions in a Manufacturing Plant. Customer
Service and Declining Product Quality. Work Force Reductions.
Environmental Pollution. Property Tax Reductions.* Ethical Analysis
and "Drawing the Line".

6   Managerial Ethics and Organizational Design   151

Ethical Codes. Ombudsman Position. Structural Causes of
Unethical Behavior. The General Electric Planning System. The
Boston Consulting Group Planning System. Impact of Planning
Systems on Managerial Behavior. Impact of Control and
Motivation Systems on Managerial Behavior. Solutions to the
Structural Causes of Unethical Behavior. The Ethical
Responsibilities of Senior Management.

CHAPTER 1

The Nature of Ethics in Management

Ethical issues occur frequently in management. They extend far beyond the commonly discussed problems of bribery, collusion, and theft, reaching into such areas as corporate acquisitions, marketing policies, and capital investments. A large corporation has taken over a smaller one through the common practice of negotiating for the purchase of stock. Then, in merging the two firms, it is found that some of the positions in one are duplicated in the other. Is it right to fire or demote executives holding those duplicate positions, many of whom have served their respective firms for years? A manufacturer that has grown rapidly in an expanding market was helped greatly during that growth by wholesale distributors that introduced its products to retail stores. Now the market has become large enough to make direct distribution from the factory to the store in truckload lots much less expensive, and the market has become competitive enough to make the cost savings from direct distribution very meaningful. Is it proper to change distribution channels? A paper company in northern Maine can generate power and reduce its energy costs by building a large dam on land that it owns, but the dam will block a river that canoeists and fishermen have used for years. Is it fair to ruin recreational opportunities for others?

"Right" and "proper" and "fair" are ethical terms. They express a judgment about behavior toward people that is felt to be just. We believe that there are right and wrong ways to behave

1

toward others, proper and improper actions, fair and unfair decisions. These beliefs are our moral standards. Moral standards differ among individuals because the values upon which they are based differ; and no one can say with certainty that a given moral standard is correct or incorrect provided it can be shown that the standard truly does express an obligation to others, and not just a benefit for ourselves. The problem is that it is difficult, even in the simplest of situations, to distinguish between "us" and "others" and between "benefits" and "obligations," and it is particularly difficult to make this distinction in business management. Why? Various groups are involved in business—managers at different levels and functions, workers of different skills and backgrounds, suppliers of different materials, distributors of different products, creditors of different types, stockholders of different holdings, and citizens of different communities, states, and countries—and a benefit for one may represent the denial of an obligation to another group.

We can illustrate this difficulty with examples from the introductory paragraph. It would seem wrong at first glance to fire executives who happened, through no fault of their own, to hold duplicate positions in the merged firms; yet let us assume that the two companies were in a very competitive industry and that the basic reason for the merger was to become more efficient and to be better able to withstand foreign competitors. What will happen if the staff reductions are not made? Who will be hurt, then, among other managers, workers, suppliers, distributors, creditors, stockholders, and members of the local communities? Who will benefit if the company is unable to survive? Even if survival is not an issue, who will benefit if the company is unable to grow or if it lacks the resources necessary for product research and market development? The basic questions are the same in the other two examples: Who will benefit, and how much? Who will be penalized, and how much? These are not easy questions to answer. In many instances, fortunately, alternatives can be considered. Duplicate managers, instead of being fired, might be retrained and reassigned. Inefficient distributors are a more difficult problem, though a place might be made for them by introducing new products or developing new markets or helping them to participate in the new distribution processes. The dam across the waterway poses the most difficult problem:

it either exists or it doesn't, and making it smaller or putting it in a different location does not really resolve the dilemma.

ETHICAL PROBLEMS AS MANAGERIAL DILEMMAS

Ethical problems are truly managerial dilemmas, because they represent a conflict between an organization's economic performance (measured by revenues, costs, and profits) and its social performance (stated in terms of obligations to persons both within and outside the organization). The nature of these obligations is, of course, open to interpretation, but most of us would agree that they include protecting loyal employees, maintaining competitive markets, and producing useful and safe products and services.

Unfortunately, the dilemma of management is that these obligations are costly, both for organizations evaluated by financial standards and for managers subject to financial controls. The manufacturer that distributes direct from the factory to stores will be more profitable and better able to withstand competition than the manufacturer that ships to wholesale warehouses for additional handling and transport. The salesperson, to use a new and more troublesome illustration, who gives small bribes to purchasing agents will have a better record and receive higher commissions than the salesperson who refuses to countenance unethical payments. The design engineer who finds ways to sharply reduce material costs is more likely to be promoted than the design engineer who places product quality and consumer safety above cost considerations. There is a "right" or "proper" or "just" balance between economic performance and social performance, and the dilemma of management comes in finding it. The purpose of this book is to examine the factors that enter into that balance and to consider various theoretical structures—economic theories, legal regulations, and philosophic doctrines—that may assist management in determining it.

It is possible, of course, to ignore the balance between economic and social performance and to argue that the managerial dilemma does not exist. This argument has been advanced from two opposite directions. Some contend that management should concentrate entirely on economic performance. This view is almost a caricature of the 19th-century approach to business, in which coal mines were assumed to be unsafe and steel mills were expected to produce pollution as well as profits. Fortunately, this belief seems to be not at all common today; most managers recognize the impact of their decisions and actions upon the organization and the community. Some people may wish that the managers made other decisions or took other actions, but I think that it is necessary to admit that the recognition exists. There are few executives active now in business firms or non-profit institutions who do not understand the far reaching consequences of their decisions and, to some extent, act upon that understanding.

The second view, which is far more widespread, comes from an oversimplification of the issue of social performance. Those who hold this view might say, for example, with some degree of asperity, that "no company should discharge harmful wastes, pay illegal bribes, or produce unsafe products" and might then declare, with an equal degree of satisfaction, that "those ethical difficulties have been resolved—let us go on to the more interesting and nationally critical problems of the proper distribution of our scarce resources." This view ignores the subtlety of ethical issues in management; it assumes that ethical questions have only a "yes" side and a "no" side and that explicit economic benefits and social costs are associated with each of these two alternatives, so that only a very simple level of moral understanding is needed to make the proper choice. In fact, however, ethical questions can have many alternatives, each with different economic and social consequences, some with unknown probabilities of occurrence, and most with personal impacts upon the managers. Let us look at some of these more complex ethical problems.

AN ETHICAL DILEMMA IN ENVIRONMENTAL PROTECTION

The exhaust from a diesel engine contains approximately 900 chemical compounds. Most of these compounds have been identified, but the environmental effects of only a few of these compounds have been studied. It seems safe to assume that some of the chemical compounds in diesel exhaust are harmful to human health or to air quality. It also seems safe to assume that in total the exhaust from a diesel engine is less harmful than that from a gasoline motor due to the absence of lead compounds—there is some lead even in "lead-free gasoline"—and to the lower levels of nitrous oxides. Every diesel engine manufacturer has a laboratory group that is studying the impact of the exhaust gases upon the general ecological system. Let us assume that in one of these companies this laboratory group finds that a particular compound is very deleterious to roadside vegetation. What are the managers of that company to do?

The managers of this diesel engine manufacturer have a number of choices, all with very uncertain outcomes, that interrelate economic, social, environmental, and personal factors. If they stop producing diesel engines, they will harm their own employees, suppliers, dealers, customers, and owners, and they will probably cause even greater deterioration in air quality as gasoline engines replace the discontinued diesel units. If they develop, at considerable cost, a catalytic converter to reduce or eliminate the harmful compound and then raise their prices, they may be less able to compete within the market. If they absorb the costs of the catalytic converter as a contribution to national welfare, the reduced profits would probably cause increased resistance in labor wage negotiations. In any case, is it ethical to shift the burden from society in general to these workers in particular? "Aha," you retort, "that will not be necessary; the managers can certainly advise the responsible people within the federal government and allow a regulatory agency to establish industry-wide standards, so that all producers will compete with the same cost and price structure." Fine, but now what is to be done about the international market? Forty percent of the diesel engines manufactured in the United States are sold abroad or are installed in domestic equipment that is then sold abroad. If these standards are extended internationally for U.S. producers, they will probably be unable to compete abroad, with all the consequences of that inability upon economies of scale and costs of production for the domestic market. If these standards are not extended internationally for U.S. producers, an implicit statement is made that foreign people are of less worth than people in the United States.

Ethical issues are complex. Let us look at one or two others. Fortunately, these problems are interesting as well as intricate.

AN ETHICAL DILEMMA IN FOREIGN BRIBERY

Bribery is generally considered reprehensible. Even in countries where it is alleged to be common, most people deplore it, except at the lower levels of some governmental bureaucracies where bribes are regarded as part of the compensation system, almost on a level with commissions or gratuities. Probably the principal reason for the widespread condemnation of bribery is its inherent inequity; it is obviously unfair to have special payments and secret influence decide issues that should be decided on their merits. All ethical systems recognize the need for equity; all ethical systems deplore the practice of bribery. It is interesting to note that the earliest written ethical belief, *The Dialogues of Plato,* discusses bribery and recognized the dilemma that an act which is prima facie—that is, at first glance, before considering the full ramifications—considered to be wrong, such as bribery, can result in ends which are prima facie considered to be good, such as the release of prisoners. This same dilemma, though perhaps on a less dramatic scale, exists in management.

Let us look first at a small and almost routine transaction. Assume that the manager of a Brazilian subsidiary of an American company has received a notice that a shipment of repair parts has been received at the São Paulo docks and is being held by the customs officials. The common practice is to hire a Brazilian agent who specializes in clearing imports through customs; such agents are considered semi-professionals, with some legal and financial training, but they are known primarily for their good verbal abilities and their superb negotiating skills. They tend to be quick-witted people who understand the interests of their opponents, and they strive for fast determination of the applicable import fees and an early release of the impounded goods. After a shipment has been cleared through customs, the agent submits a bill that includes an amount for the duty and a charge for the negotiations. This charge varies, but not with the size of the duty: a commission at a set percentage would be considered "unethical" in Brazil. It is the agent's duty to negotiate the lowest possible fees, and it is considered wrong to force people to choose between their own interests and those of their client. Instead, the charge depends on the time needed to complete the transaction: the quicker the work, the higher the payment. It is assumed that part of the agent's fee has been paid to the customs officials; the larger payments, of course, bring more prompt attention from the officials and much quicker release of the goods. Payments on this basis also serve the interests of the client, for delays in Brazilian customs can extend from two to three months.

In this example, the ethical issue is slightly blurred, partially because there is no proof that bribery payments have been made—though it is logical to assume that some exchange has occurred to gain the attention of the customs officials—and partially because this exchange has been indirect. Managers in the subsidiary of the American company can claim legally that they have not paid bribes, though I am not certain that this claim would be considered defensible by those of us outside the courtroom. The ethical problem, though blurred, seems clear enough: Should a company employ an agent who will probably bribe a government official, resulting in inequitable treatment for others and favored treatment for itself?

Most ethical issues in management are at this apparently simple level: there is a dichotomous, yes or no choice, with relatively clear financial benefits and social obligations associated with each alternative, and the solution proposed is to sensitize people trained in financial analysis to recognize and include social costs in that analysis. But, as stated earlier, this seems to oversimplify the ethical dilemma and to ignore many of the complexities of managerial ethics.

Let us add some of those complexities to the present illustration. Let us assume that the repair parts in question are needed to maintain a communication system, or a manufacturing plant, or even a health-care facility. If the parts are not cleared promptly through customs and a breakdown occurs, people may be inconvenienced because of a failure of the communication system, or they may be unemployed because of a shutdown of the manufacturing plant, or they may suffer death or severe pain because of a breakdown in service at a hospital. Now it becomes clear that the comparison of financial benefits versus social costs is neither as simple nor as obvious as it appeared earlier, for the social ramifications of the decision extend beyond the first level of results into subsequent levels. The consequences of managerial decisions, even on such day-to-day issues as the customs clearance of imported goods, extend throughout society, and these consequences, both positive and negative, have to be included in the original analysis.

Let us also agree that the problem being discussed, paying an indirect bribe for prompt customs clearance, is not truly dichotomous. Numerous alternatives in addition to the obvious yes and no choices are also available. The subsidiary could engage in forward planning and order repair parts far in advance of actual need so that the lengthy delays in customs could be tolerated and the need to pay bribes eliminated. Statistical analysis of the operations, whether of a communication system, a manufacturing plant, or a health-care facility, would indicate a probable demand for repair parts, and numerous mathematical models are available to establish adequate inventory levels, given lengthy delivery times. Another alternative would be to have a corporate attorney negotiate with the customs officials, subject to explicit policy instructions not to pay bribes under any circumstances, and force the officials through legal penalties to clear shipments in the order of their arrival. Yet another alternative would be to obtain repair parts from local suppliers, thus helping to bolster the national economy while avoiding the problems of customs clearance entirely.

Each of these alternatives has a financial cost that we can assume will be somewhat greater than the expenses for the currently minimal bribes, but that cost can be computed. So, on the surface, it would appear that we are now looking at a comparison of financial costs versus social benefits. But, to the manager who has to decide, it is very obvious that here each alternative has a social cost that is more subtle. The inventory models require, for computation, an estimate of the costs of lacking a part that is needed for repairs. The original intent of the management scientists who developed these models was to consider only objective judgments of the costs to the company, but it has become obvious in recent years that the models also have to include subjective estimates of the costs to the employees, the customer, and the general population. Even unsophisticated management-science procedures now require some estimate of the costs external to the firm and of the economic damages caused by the firm. In the particular instance being discussed, what cost should be included for Brazilian people who are being inconvenienced when their communication system breaks down due to lack of repair parts? What cost should be included for Brazilian workers who become unemployed and unpaid when their factory is shut down? What cost should be included for Brazilian patients who are untreated when their hospital is unable to function? These are not simple financial estimates; they are extended social costs that are difficult to compute but have to be included in ethical managerial decisions, even when management-science procedures are being used. Ethical managerial issues are also posed by the other two alternatives that were suggested—employing a corporate attorney to force the customs official to adhere to the provisions of the law even if this resulted in court actions and civil penalties against those officials, and purchasing repair parts within the country, even if this required an uneconomic transfer of both capital and technology to a local company. If the former alternative were chosen, a corporate attorney would be hired to impose American standards of bureaucratic integrity upon the Brazilian civil service. At one level, there is the question whether an American firm has the right to force its views upon others. At a more subtle level, we have to look at the social structure of Brazil. Corporate attorneys there tend to come from the wealthier families, while customs officials are members of a much poorer class. In essence, the company would be transferring payments from the poor to the rich and thereby helping to maintain the inequitable social divisions of South America.

The sourcing of repair parts within the country seems an attractive alternative superficially, but it involves moving jobs from the United States to Brazil, along with the proprietary technology and some capital investment. That movement will doubtless be directly counter to employee expectations—if not union contracts—in the United States. Until recently, union negotiators seldom foresaw the possibility of foreign purchase of complex components, believing the necessary technical skills to be absent in low-wage-rate areas. With the continual development of advanced technologies in less developed countries that situation has changed. Using foreign labor may create worker hardships in the United States.

Having examined the extended impacts, multiple alternatives, and mixed outcomes that seem to be inherently associated with ethical decisions in management, we will now consider two additional levels of complexity, and then it will be possible to present a series of conclusions on the nature of ethics in management. The fourth level of complexity is the uncertain consequences of managerial decisions. When a managerial decision is made, it is seldom clear exactly what the outcome of that decision will be, and unfortunately the greatest clarity often seems to be linked to the least ethical action, judged by prima facie standards. In the simple illustration that has been used throughout this section—the payment of an indirect bribe to facilitate the clearance of repair parts through customs—it is reasonable to assume that if the bribe is paid, the shipment will be released.

The Brazilian customs officials may be unfamiliar with the cynical 19th-century American aphorism, "An honest man is one who, once purchased, stays bought." However, they doubtless understand that unless agreements concluded with the import agents are observed (one hesitates to say "honored" in this context), further negotiations and payments will be impaired. An equal certainty does not extend to the other alternatives.

Uncertainty is even present in the alternative of an expanded repair parts inventory. We have all been annoyed by delays in repair service caused by inadequate inventories; such inadequacies can stem from management inattention, financial constraints, or pure chance. Most of them can probably be ascribed to the first two causes, but a combination of rare events is always a possibility, particularly in repair service where numerous parts are needed for each operating system, where a given region or area contains multiple operating systems, and where obtaining repair parts is subject to extensive delays. Murphy's Law has not been repealed by management science, it has just been partially circumvented; and even large, economically unjustifiable inventories cannot prevent downtime caused by a lack of parts. This is the dilemma that the manager of every repair service intuitively understands: he or she is unable to assure complete protection against failure. That inability is annoying when the parts are needed by a communication system, troublesome when they are needed by a manufacturing plant, and depressing when they are needed by a hospital.

Formal procedures for including uncertainty are available for inventory-planning models, based upon the statistical analysis of historical operating patterns, but such procedures are not applicable to the other two alternatives that were suggested, since relevant data are lacking. It is not at all clear what would happen if an attorney threatened or instituted legal action against customs officials in Brazil. Those officials might release the shipments promptly to avoid harassment in a legal system they did not understand—or papers might be lost, hearings delayed, and shipments misdirected as the same officials created havoc in an import system they understood very well.

An incident illustrates how the legal system can be confounded. I have been told that a Brazilian attorney watched customs officials unwrap, inspect, and clear for import 20 fuel injectors for large diesel engines. The fuel injector is a precisely machined component in the engine; it tends to wear out because of the high pressures that are required in operation. The fuel injectors were inspected, cleared, shipped, and stored. After the first one was installed on an engine, it was found that a pinch of very fine sand had been deposited in the input ports of each unit. All of them had to be scrapped. Sabotage is not common, in Brazil or elsewhere, but it does happen; a manager has to recognize that it can occur and plan for that possibility.

It is also not at all clear what would happen if a local company were selected and trained to produce the needed repair parts inside the country. The training would probably extend far beyond simple instruction in manual skills, requiring the importation of advanced equipment for both production and testing and the explanation of managerial processes in operations scheduling, test evaluation, and quality control. Despite technological and financial assistance from the parent firm, and assuming goodwill and effort on the part of all others, the exportation of highly technical processes is often unsuccessful; it requires a degree of precision and skill that may be outside the culture of the receiving firm.

In summary, it is not certain that the necessary repair parts can be manufactured in Brazil, despite the investment of money and effort. It is also not certain that they can be imported into Brazil by pressuring the customs officials with legal penalties. It is, however, reasonably certain that these parts can be received promptly by employing an import agent and authorizing the customary payments. Uncertainty seems to be a constant companion of the ethical approach to management.

The last level of complexity that we will consider is the personal involvement of the managers. It seems reasonable to assume that this involvement is partially an emotional concern with the ethical dilemma—no one likes to pay bribes or to conspire in their indirect payment—but that it is primarily a practical worry over the impact of ethical issues upon the manager's salary, promotion, and career. Managers, particularly those in autonomous operating units some distance from the corporate headquarters, are expected to "get things done" and to "keep things running." They are not told that they are free to do whatever is necessary to accomplish those goals, and many corporations have codes of ethics and specific functional policies that attempt to preclude many actions, but the managerial controls tend to emphasize financial results and not ethical decisions. The ability of managers to "keep things running" will show up on the control system during the next quarter, while the decisions and actions that enabled them to do so have to be explained only verbally, if at all. Managerial controls tend to focus on the short term and the obvious but they are often used in judgments about longer-term salaries and promotions.

Managers in almost all companies operate within the constraints of a control system. Certainly, managers in all well-run companies operate within such constraints, and it does no harm to assume that the American manufacturing firm with a troubled subsidiary in Brazil is well run. The controls are normally based upon a comparison of actual results with planned objectives. These objectives are usually set by an extrapolation of past results, with some adjustment for current conditions and local problems derived through discussions between the responsible managers. Both results and objectives are focused primarily on financial measures such as sales revenues, variable costs, fixed expenses, and the resultant profits or losses, because those are the figures that are available from the accounting records. Assuming that the Brazilian subsidiary has this kind of control system, that failure to provide adequate repair service will eventually affect sales revenues, and assuming that payments to the import agent can be classified as a legitimate and necessary business expense, it must be a rare manager who would not say, "Damn the company for putting me into this position," and make the call authorizing indirect payments. This is unfortunate, but it happens, and I think that it is necessary to understand the behavioral implications of the control system that helps to make it happen.

CHARACTERISTICS OF ETHICAL PROBLEMS IN MANAGEMENT

What does all this mean? We have examined in great detail a relatively minor problem faced by a worried manager primarily to consider in detail the actual nature of the ethical dilemma in management. From that examination, five conclusions concerning the complexity of managerial ethics can be stated simply and directly:

1. Most ethical decisions have extended consequences. The results of managerial decisions and actions do not stop with the first-level consequences. Rather, these results extend throughout society, and that extension constitutes the essence of the ethical argument: the decisions of managers have an impact upon others—both within the organization and within the society—that is beyond their control and that therefore should be considered when the decisions are made. Bribes change governmental processes. Pollution affects environmental health. Unsafe products destroy individual lives. There is little disagreement here; most people recognize the extended consequences of managerial actions. The disagreement results from the existence of the multiple alternatives, mixed outcomes, uncertain occurrences, and personal implications that complicate the decision process leading to those actions.

2. Most ethical decisions have multiple alternatives. It is commonly thought that ethical issues in management are primarily dichotomous, a yes and a no choice but no other alternatives. Should a manager pay a bribe or not? Should a factory pollute the air or not? Should a company manufacture unsafe products or not? Although a dichotomous framework presents the ethical issues in sharp contrast, it does not accurately reflect the managerial dilemma. As has been seen in the simple illustration of bribery payments for import clearances, and as will be shown in numerous other examples throughout this text, multiple alternatives have to be considered in making ethical choices.

3. Most ethical decisions have mixed outcomes. It is commonly thought that ethical issues in management are largely antithetical, with directly opposed financial returns and social costs. Pay an indirect bribe, but maintain the sales volume of imported goods through prompt delivery. Cause some air or water pollution, but avoid the costs of installing and operating pollution-control equipment. Design a slightly unsafe product, but reduce the material and labor costs of manufacture. Like the dichotomous framework, the antithetical model for outcome evaluation presents the ethical issues in sharp focus but does not accurately portray the managerial dilemma. Social benefits and costs as well as financial revenues and expenses are associated with almost all of the alternatives in ethical choices.

4. Most ethical decisions have uncertain consequences. It is commonly thought that ethical issues in management are free of risk or doubt, with a known outcome for each alternative. Pay the bribe, and receive the imported goods promptly. Invest in pollution-control equipment, and the emissions will be reduced X percent at Y costs of operation. Produce an absolutely safe product at an additional cost of Z dollars per unit. A deterministic model—that is, one without probabilities—simplifies the process of analysis, but it does not accurately describe the managerial dilemma. It was not at all clear what consequences would follow from the alternatives considered to avoid paying indirect bribes to Brazilian customs officials; it is not all clear what consequences will follow from most ethical choices.

5. Most ethical decisions have personal implications. It is commonly thought that ethical issues in management are largely impersonal, divorced from the lives and careers of the managers. Many people believe that prima facie ethical decisions in a given operation may reduce the profits of the company but not the executives' salaries or their opportunities for promotion. Managerial controls, however, are designed to record financial results of the operations, not the ethical quality of the decisions that led to those results, and most incentive systems are based upon these controls. Maintain the dollar sales of imported goods at expected levels, and despite slightly increased expenses for indirect bribes, the quarterly review will be pleasant and remunerative. Delay the installation of pollution-control equipment, and the return on invested capital will be close to the planned percentage. Redesign the product to reduce material and labor costs, and profit margins and the chances of promotion will increase. An impersonal model certainly simplifies the process of decision on ethical issues, but it far from accurately describes the managerial dilemma. Individual benefits and costs, as well as financial and social benefits and costs, are associated with most of the alternatives in ethical decisions.

EXAMPLES OF ETHICAL PROBLEMS IN MANAGEMENT

Ethical problems in management are complex because of the extended consequences, multiple alternatives, mixed outcomes, uncertain occurrences, and personal implications. Ethical problems in management are also pervasive, because managers make decisions and take actions that will affect other people. If those decisions and actions affect other people adversely, if they hurt or harm those people in ways beyond their individual control, then we have an ethical problem that requires some degree of moral analysis in addition to the more common economic analysis. What are some of these ethical problems? Let us look at a few, bearing in mind that the moral content of each differs, and that each of us will differ in our view of the moral severity of that content. That is, using the issues discussed in the introductory paragraph of this chapter, some of us may feel that it is morally wrong to discharge long-service employees following a merger, to replace wholesale distributors as the market matures, or to build a power-generating dam that will block recreational access to a river. Others of us may feel that some decisions of this kind are morally wrong but that others—particularly the dam on company-owned property—are morally right. Still other people may argue that while these decisions have unfortunate consequences, they are nonetheless all morally right.

Moral standards differ between individuals because the ethical systems of belief—the values or priorities, the convictions that people think are truly important and upon which their moral standards are based—also differ. These beliefs depend upon each person's family background, cultural heritage, church association, educational experience, and other factors. The differences in ethical beliefs are not important at this stage of the discussion; they will be examined in the next three chapters. What is important at this stage is to recognize that each of the decisions and actions that will be described briefly below can affect other people adversely, can hurt or harm them in ways beyond their control, and consequently, have a moral content. The condition of hurt or harm to others in ways beyond their control is the essential element in the ethical dilemma of management. That condition is present in all the examples that follow.

Before going on to describe these additional ethical problems in management, let me state two qualifications and provide a personal explanation. First, the intent is not to describe every possible instance in which managerial decisions and actions can hurt or harm individuals in ways beyond their control. Rather, the intent is to provide a limited number of examples that show the pervasive nature of ethical problems in management and furnish general topics for subsequent discussion of the various analytical means for reaching decisions when confronted with such problems.

Second, the intent is not to describe dramatic and well-publicized instances of management decisions that were clearly unethical and often illegal as well. The president of Lockheed did pay $3.2 million to various government officials and representatives of the prime minister of Japan to ensure the purchase of 20 passenger planes by the Japanese national airline.[1] Senior members of management at General Dynamics did add $63 million of improper overhead expenses, including country club memberships and dog kennel fees, to defense contracts during the period 1979–82.[2] Regional managers at E. F. Hutton did issue bank overdrafts that gave Hutton the interest-free use of up to $250 million and cost banks as much as $8 million.[3] Marketing executives at a company manufacturing artificial eye lenses for cataract-replacement surgery did, according to a report issued by a subcommittee of Congress, provide "free use of a yacht off Florida, travel in Europe, all-expense paid and week-long training seminars in the Bahamas, second homes, and cash rebates" for buying their lenses rather than the lenses of their competitors.[4] These unethical actions did occur, but few people would defend them except perhaps to say that one has to adopt foreign business practices when doing business abroad, or that the Defense Department is too large to be properly managed, or that the banks should have recognized what was happening much earlier, or that health-care costs are clearly out of control. The intent here is to look not at such actions, but at a range of issues at the operating, middle, and strategic levels of management and in most of the functional and technical specialties. Some of these issues require decisions by senior executives, but most are the routine, even mundane decisions and actions that lower-level managers—and recent graduates of business schools—face on an almost daily basis.

Last, and this is the personal explanation, I am going to use anonymous quotations to amplify and support some of the descriptions of ethical problems in management. This is in direct contradiction to the research rule that sources should always be cited, so that the validity of the findings can be substantiated. However, I believe that in this instance the use of anonymous quotations may be justified. It is difficult to get examples of ethical problems at the lower and middle levels of management. Managers at those levels do not like to discuss the ethical dilemmas they have faced, for the obvious reason that those discussions can adversely affect their careers. They will discuss them only with persons who are known to have an interest in the area, who perhaps can help them in the resolution of the problem, and who certainly will maintain confidentiality. I have taught at three schools of business administration over the past 12 years, and at each of these institutions I have either conducted short seminars or used short cases in elective classes that revealed my interest in the ethics of management. Former students from those seminars and classes occasionally contact me when troubled about particular practices that seem to be accepted as ordinary business routines within their companies. They write or speak with the assumption of confidentiality, and so I cannot identify them. Yet their descriptions are much more vivid, and probably valid, than my own because they have been part of the problems they are describing, and so I wish to include the descriptions. That is the reason I believe the use of anonymous quotations is justified in these examples. Now, on to the problems.

Pricing Level

Price, it would seem, should be a purely economic decision based upon cost and demand. Yet the pricing level selected can have harmful effects upon some customers. In banking, for example, under the combined impact of deregulation by the government and competition from other financial-service firms, it has become common to pay fairly high rates of interest on customer deposits. But the benefits of those rates go primarily to the customers with the larger bank balances. To offset the increased interest that must be paid to attract the larger deposits and to reflect the actual costs of service, most banks have raised the fees they charge smaller customers.

> I have been asked to do a study of the pricing for our checking account services. Other banks in the area now charge $0.10 for each transaction for accounts that don't maintain a $1,000.00 balance and an additional $5.00 per month for the very small accounts with a balance that falls under $300.00. That makes a lot of sense, economically. We just barely break even now servicing the medium-sized accounts, and we lose money on the smaller ones. The proposed price changes would mean that our returns would be equal for all three sizes of accounts.

But there is a problem. We are an urban bank. Many of our customers are retired, on Social Security. Five dollars a month is a major expense for them; it represents a couple of meals that they are not going to eat. Most of them don't have the money to maintain a $300 balance. They're older, and frightened of carrying cash. I don't think that it is right to, in essence, deny checking account services to older people, but I don't know what to do about it. You see, if we don't have the same rate structure as the other banks, we will get all of these older and unprofitable customers.

When I left [name of the business school], I was determined that I would maintain my personal standards in everything that I did. Yet in the first year I am going to recommend a policy that I think is morally wrong. (Statement of former student)

Advertising Messages

Truth in advertising is a complex issue, and an emotional one. A rigidly truthful television or magazine ad, every statement of which is supported by a reference to a scientific study, would be incredibly dull and probably ineffective. A totally untruthful television or magazine ad, with wildly exaggerated claims, would be illegal and probably equally ineffective. Varying degrees of truthfulness and deception lie between those two extremes. The problem for one former student was where to draw the line along that spectrum.

Despite our reputation as hucksters, 90 percent of what we do in advertising is legitimate, and based upon valid market analysis. For the large majority of our clients, we act more as marketing consultants than as advertisers. Our ads may be dull; they are generally unimaginative; and they often present a very one-sided view of things, but they are seldom designed to be deliberately untruthful.

It's the other 10 percent that I worry about. We have a client who says that they want a campaign with more "bite"; bite to them means more pull, more attraction to the buyer, even if that attraction is blatantly untrue and totally misrepresented. They are in the financial-services industry, but they want to sell their products as if they were headache remedies or arthritis rubs. "Up 387 percent over the past three years" is the heading they have on a mutual fund ad, and that is an accurate statement only if you stay strictly within that time frame; over the past five years the fund has not kept pace with the growth in the Dow Jones Averages. "8½ percent interest" is the heading they have on a money market fund;

there is a small asterisk, and down at the bottom of the page a footnote that explains the 8½ percent is for the first month only. "Insured by [name of an insurance company]" is a phrase they want on every ad that mentions customer accounts; that insurance company is their wholly owned and poorly funded subsidiary. We do the work for them, but I don't like it. (Statement of former student)

Product Promotions

Advertising is one form of promotion; another is the use of "free" gifts and price rebates to attract customers. Under the impact of deregulation, airlines have developed product promotions in the form of additional flights and vacation lodgings for "frequent flyers"—passengers who exceed a given mileage on a particular airline each year. Most of the frequent flyers travel on business, yet the benefits are given to the traveler who decides what airline will be used, not to the company that generates the volume of traffic and pays for the tickets, and the cost of those benefits is borne by the nonbusiness traveler, who generally flies much less often and is usually much less able to bear the additional expense.

> There are executives in our company who will select a flight based upon the frequent flyer benefits, not upon the cost to the company or the time spent in the air. The man for whom I work is probably the greatest offender; he gets me and others, when we fly, to use his card so that he accumulates the mileage, and the freebies.
>
> Our company has a corporate code of conduct, and the chairman gets us all together once a year and talks about the high standards of [name of the company], yet here is an executive ripping everybody off, and nobody cares. Probably the chairman approves; he always uses one of the corporate jets for his own vacation travel. (Statement of former student)

Working Conditions

The working conditions for many manual and clerical employees are less than ideal. Temperature, humidity, or noise levels may be too high; ventilation and lighting may be too low, and fumes and dust are still found in some workplaces. The most harmful of these conditions along with the obvious safety hazards, have been outlawed by state and federal laws, but there are still many

opportunities to improve working conditions for hourly employees. Here is a former student who felt that it would harm his
career to make such improvements.

> I think that all MBAs, and I'll include the BBAs too, should be
> forced as part of their education to work in a steel stamping plant
> or a grey iron foundry. The noise, the heat, the fumes, and the
> pace of work are close to intolerable. If there aren't enough places
> for all of them in a stamping plant or an iron foundry, you could
> put the balance of them "out on the line" [on the assembly line in
> an automobile factory].
>
> We have executives in this company who just don't understand
> what it is like to work under these conditions. Their offices are in
> New York, and they only come out here a couple of times a year to
> tell us that we're falling behind on the profit plan. I could put in a
> capital request to improve some of the worst conditions, but I
> would have to fight to get it approved. I'm not certain I want to
> make that effort; people who fight for capital projects that don't
> show a substantial internal rate of return tend not to get promoted
> around here. (Statement of former student)

Customer Service

Declining product quality has been a problem in many industries
for a number of years. Declining product quality in the automobile industry results in "lemons," new cars with major defects
that can create substantial hardships for the buyers, who cannot
depend upon these cars for transportation to and from work or
to and from medical appointments, shopping trips, family gath-
erings, and so on.

> I work in the marketing department at [name of an auto com-
> pany], calling on dealers. Customers with mechanical problems on
> new cars are supposed to go first to the dealer, then to the com-
> pany, and finally, if both of those fail, to an arbitration program set
> up by the Better Business Bureaus in each state. But these proce-
> dures don't work. The dealer is paid only a portion of the full cost
> of warranty repairs, so he tries to get by, doing as little work as
> possible. I can authorize additional work, but the money comes out
> of my budget, and you can't run over the budget too often. The
> result is that the major problems on a customer's car, where we
> ought to just replace the motor or the transmission or the electrical
> system, never really do get fixed. We only fix the minor ones.
> (Statement of former student)

Work Force Reductions

It has become common to reduce the size and the overhead cost of many large companies by discharging some of the employees, to create a "lean and mean" style of management. These "downsizing operations" are generally a response to an increase in competitive pressures, but there is an obvious human cost to the people forced to leave.

> Our company, in August, is going to announce the firing of 24,000 workers, including 15,000 administrative employees. [Name of the company] has always had a reputation for job security, almost lifetime employment, so this announcement is going to come as a shock to many people.
>
> Of course, the older ones will get the option of early retirement. But the younger ones, in their 30s and 40s, are just going to get a few months' severance pay and some outplacement counseling. I am part of a task force that was set up to decide exactly what benefits should be given to the various longevity classes.
>
> The senior executives in this company had it easy. When they were at this level, the only problem they had was expansion: finding more people, training them, promoting them. They never had to deal with contraction; they don't recognize the really agonizing nature of the decisions we have to make on an almost daily basis now. (Statement of former student)

Environmental Pollution

Improper disposal of toxic wastes is clearly illegal, yet some companies continue to dump chemicals, despite possible harm to the environment and probable conflict with the law.

> I have been working for [name of the company] for about six months, at their [name of the city] plant. It is common practice here to pour used solvents and cleaning solutions down the storm drain. I asked the plant manager about it, and he said that this is legal in small amounts. I don't think that it is legal, and I don't think that the amounts are that small, but I'm not certain that I want to get involved at this stage of my career. (Statement of former student)

Community Relations

The major employer within a local community has substantial economic power, particularly if the employer has plants in other locations and can move work, and employment, among plants. This economic power often is used in pressing for tax reductions, which can have an obvious impact upon residents of the community by increasing their taxes or decreasing their services.

[Name of the company] is pushing for a 76 percent tax reduction in [name of the city], where I live. Two years ago it got a 24 percent reduction. Now it is threatening to close the plant unless it gets the full amount. If that reduction goes through, it is going to increase taxes on my house by over $500 a year. I can afford it; I'm well paid. But there are older people around here, and some farmers, who are going to be driven right to the wall. Doesn't the company understand what it is doing? (Statement of former student)

Supplier Relations

Large manufacturing firms have economic power within the communities in which they operate, and against the small suppliers from which they purchase materials, parts, and supplies. Economic power is a difficult concept to define, but it is an easy force to recognize.

This company has started to play hardball with our suppliers. People in purchasing think nothing of calling up a supplier we've worked with for years, and telling the supplier it has lost the business unless we get a 7 percent price reduction. Generally we can't make the parts at the prices that purchasing demands, so it is an empty threat. But the supplier doesn't know that; they'll come back with a 3 percent reduction, we'll compromise eventually at 4.2 percent, but we've started to drive somebody else out of business. (Statement of former student)

ANALYSIS OF ETHICAL PROBLEMS IN MANAGEMENT

How do we decide on these and other ethical issues? You may regard some of the examples cited as simple instances of practical management—small suppliers to any large manufacturing company have to be competitive in their price quotations and quality standards, or they will lose the business, and this is particularly true of suppliers to the automobile companies attempting to meet foreign competition. You may regard others as outrageous abuses of power and position—it is hard to justify a

76 percent tax reduction for a corporation that will substantially increase the taxes for community residents, assuming that the original assessments were made equitably. Ethical decisions are easy to make when a person is not directly involved. From a distance, it is easy to review other people's actions and say, "Yes, that is right," or "No, that is wrong."

Ethical decisions are much more difficult to make when a person is directly involved in the situation. Put yourself in the position of the purchasing agent in the automobile company who had to lie to a supplier. Could you do it? If you did not do it, could you continue to work for that company? Put yourself in the position of the person who discovered that the company he worked for was pouring solvents and cleaning fluids down the drain. What would you do?

Suppose you were the former student whose immediate superior required her to cheat the company when purchasing airline tickets, and pass along the benefits to him. Would you do it? This is not truly an ethical dilemma, for there is no conflict between the economic and social performance of the company. This is just a simple case of managerial dishonesty, but your career is probably at risk, and not just if you "blow the whistle" on your boss. At some time in the future, a corporate auditor may find out about this practice and list you as one of the participants.

Suppose you were the former student who had to decide on the proper pricing level for the checking account services offered by your bank. Now, how to you analyze the situation? Is it strictly a matter of costs and margins, or does the bank have some obligation to continue to provide checking account services to older members of the community, and do you have some obligation to make certain that that occurs? Suppose you were asked to set up policy guidelines for the employees to be discharged in a corporate downsizing operation; what standards would you use? Suppose you recognized that your company was producing unsafe products, or making illegal payments; how would you decide what action to take? You need a method of analysis, beyond your intuitive moral standards, when confronted with an immediate ethical problem.

Ethical decisions are not simple choices between right and wrong; they are complex judgments on the balance between the economic performance and the social performance of an organization. In all the instances described above, except for the managerial dishonesty in the example of the airline tickets, the economic performance of the organization, measured by revenues, costs, and profits, will be improved. In all the instances described above, the social performance of the organization— much more difficult to measure, but expressed as obligations to managers, workers, customers, suppliers, distributors, and members of the local community—will be reduced. People are going to be hurt. There has to be a balance between economic and social performance. How do you reach this balance? Three methods of analysis are relevant: economic, legal, and ethical.

Economic Analysis

It is possible to look at many of the problems that have been described as having a definite ethical content from the point of view of microeconomic theory, relying on impersonal market forces to make the decision between economic and social performance. Work force reductions and plant closings are admittedly unpleasant for the workers who lose their jobs, but there is a labor market, and these workers will be employed again, provided they are willing to adjust their wage demands to market conditions. The small wholesalers that are going to be replaced by direct factory shipments to retail stores doubtless feel troubled, but their costs are too high; bring those costs down to a competitive level, and they will not be replaced. The underlying belief is that a market economy has a limited number of resources and that when consumers are supplied with highest-quality goods at lowest possible costs, then those resources are being used as efficiently and effectively as possible.

Legal Analysis

It is also possible to look at each of the problems that have an ethical content using the framework of legal theory, relying on impersonal social forces to make the choice between "right" and "wrong." Work force reductions and plant closings are unpleasant, but society has never felt that they were so harmful to the people involved that a law prohibiting them was required. Should they become a major problem, a law can be passed to deal with the situation. The small wholesalers that are going to be replaced doubtless feel badly, but they may have an implicit contract from their earlier service. They can sue in a court of law; if they win, they will not be replaced. The underlying belief here is that a democratic society can establish its own rules and that if people and organizations follow those rules, then members of that society will be treated as justly as possible.

Ethical Analysis

Lastly, it is possible to look at each of the problems that have a moral content using the structure of normative philosophy, relying on basic principles to make the choice between "right" and "wrong." Work force reductions and plant closings, again, are unpleasant, but we can compute "the greatest good for the greatest number" and decide on that basis. The small wholesalers that are to be replaced are unhappy, but we can set up a rule that every organization, faced with an equivalent situation, has to act in the same way—Kant's Categorical Imperative—and thus achieve consistent and equitable behavior. The belief underlying normative philosophy is that if all the rational men and women in a society acted on the same principles of either beneficiency or consistency, then members of that society would be treated as fairly as possible.

Three methods of analysis have been proposed to resolve ethical dilemmas in management. The next three chapters will examine these methods in considerably greater detail.

Footnotes

1. "Japan: An Aftershock of the Lockheed Affair," *Business Week*, April 12, 1976, p. 43.

2. Roger Bennett, "Profile of Harry Crown, Founder of General Dynamics, Inc.," *New York Times*, June 16, 1985, p. 26f.

3. Scott McMurray, "Battered Broker: E.F. Hutton Appears Headed for Long Seige in Bank-Draft Scheme," *The Wall Street Journal*, July 12, 1985, p. lf.

4. *Ann Arbor News*, July 19, 1985, p. B1.

CASES

Forestry Equipment Company

The Forestry Equipment Company was founded in 1955 to produce a new machine that would permit the recovery and sale of the waste products at a sawmill. When a round log is cut into square lumber, the outer portions of the wood, termed slabs and edgings, are surplus. In the 19th and early 20th centuries, when sawmilling was a major industry in the United States, these slabs and edgings were burned in a boiler to produce steam power for the mill; with the extension of electrical service to rural areas in the 1930s and 1940s, it became cheaper to purchase power, and the slabs and edgings became complete waste products that had to be disposed of through open-air burning or dumping at a landfill. Since the slabs and edgings represent 20 percent to 25 percent of the content of the logs by weight, this disposal represented a considerable problem and expense for the mills.

Many persons, particularly those associated with the various conservation groups, had suggested that the slabs and edgings might be chipped, or reduced into pieces about five-eighth inch by one inch by one inch through a mechanical knife action, and then sold for use as pulpwood in the production of paper. The problem, however, was that the bark was still on the slabs and edgings, and the bark did not dissolve in the pulping process but remained as gritty black specks in the finished paper, which obviously detracted from the quality. The Pinchot League, an organization dedicated to the preservation of the American forests, had sponsored a contest in the early 1950s for the design of a machine to debark the slabs and edgings, but this sawmill waste is in the form of long, awkward strips of wood, with knots and root swells, that are costly to handle and difficult to debark, and no successful machines were produced.

The founder of the Forestry Equipment Company had the idea of debarking the logs before they were sawn; this would obviously reduce the handling required for the individual slabs and edgings and would also reduce many of the mechanical problems involved in the bark removal. The prototype machine was finished in the fall of 1955 and ran successfully at a sawmill in northern Maine through the winter. However, sales were not as quick to develop as had been anticipated; only 12 machines, at an average price of $12,500, were sold during 1956, and while sales increased in 1957 and 1958, the company by 1958 was just barely above break-even.

	1956	1957	1958
Company Sales	$158,000	$324,000	$575,000
Company Profits	(22,000)	(3,000)	14,000

There were a number of reasons for the disappointing growth in sales. There were 18,000 sawmills east of the Mississippi, many of which were interested in the machine as a solution to the disposal of the waste slabs and edgings and as a source of additional revenue through the sale of the pulp chips, but many of these sawmills did not have adequate cash or credit to purchase the debarkers. Also, a sawmill required a contract from a paper company to purchase the chips, but the paper companies were very hesitant to sign these contracts since they had to install expensive truck and rail car unloading equipment to handle the wood chips. (Until 1956, all pulpwood was delivered to paper mills in the form of logs cut five feet in length, to be debarked in large drums and then chipped at the mill.) Up to 1956, pulpmills in Georgia and Alabama, where there was a shortage of pulpwood, were the only ones to install unloading and handling equipment for chips, and over 100 log debarkers were sold in those two states, but two small companies started in that area to build competitive (and copied) equipment.

In 1959, one of the major paper companies in the United States, with pulpmills at three locations in the New England area, decided to conserve its own forest resources by purchasing chips from local sawmills; unloading and handling equipment was to be installed at all three pulpmills, and 120 log debarkers were to be purchased for lease to the sawmills. This action would prove the validity of the log-barking and slab-chipping concept in the eastern United States and would lead to increased sales as other paper companies followed suit. This sale of 120 machines would ensure the success of the Forestry Equipment Company; since the firm was already operating at break-even, the contributions would flow directly through to retained earnings and provide the financial basis for expansion into other sawmill and pulpmill equipment.

There was just one problem: the vice president of woodlands for the paper company wanted a guarantee that he would receive a personal payment of 5 percent of the purchase price, in cash, in return for placing the order with the Forestry Equipment Company.

Exercise. What action should the founder and general manager of the Forestry Equipment Company take in regard to the potential order for 120 log debarkers?

Sarah Goodwin

Sarah Goodwin was a 1980 graduate of an M.B.A. program. She had majored in marketing, was interested in retailing, and had been delighted to receive a job offer from a large and prestigious department store chain in northern California. The first year of employment at this chain was considered to be a training program, but formal instruction was very limited. Instead, after a tour of the facilities and a welcoming speech by the president, each of the new trainees was assigned to work as an assistant to a buyer in one of the departments. The intent was that the trainees would work with five or six buyers during the year, rotating assignments every two months, and would make themselves "useful" enough during those assignments so that at least one buyer would ask to have that person join his or her department on a permanent basis.

Buyers are critical in the management of a department store. They select the goods to be offered, negotiate purchase terms, set retail prices, arrange displays, organize promotions, and are generally responsible for the operations of the departments within the store. Each buyer acts as a profit center, and sales figures and profit margins are reported monthly to the senior executives. In this particular chain, the sales and profits were calculated on a square-foot basis (that is, per square foot of floor space occupied by the department), and the buyers contended, generally on a friendly basis, to outperform each other so that their square footage would be expanded. The buyers received substantial commissions, based upon monthly profits.

Sarah's first assignment was to work for the buyer of the gourmet food department. This was a small unit at the main store that sold packaged food items such as jams and jellies, crackers and cookies, cheese, spreads, and candies, most of which were imported from Europe. The department also offered preserved foods such as smoked fish and meats, and some expensive delicacies such as caviar, truffles, and estate-bottled wines. Many of the items were packaged as gifts, in boxes or baskets, with decorative wrappings and ties. Sarah was originally disappointed to have been sent to such a small and specialized department rather than to a larger one that dealt with more general fashion goods, but she soon found that this assignment was considered a "plum." The buyer, Maria Castellani, was a well-known personality throughout the store; witty, competent, and sarcastic, she served as a sounding board, consultant, and friend to the other buyers. She would evaluate fashions, forecast trends, chastise managers ("managers" in a department store are the people associated with finance, personnel, accounting, or planning, not merchandising), and discuss retailing events and changes in an amusing, informative way. Everybody in the store seemed to find a reason to stop by the gourmet food department at least once during each day to chat with Maria. Sarah was naturally included in these conversations, and consequently she found that she was getting to know all the other buyers and could ask one of them to request her as an assistant at the next rotation of assignments.

For the first five weeks of her employment, Sarah was exceptionally happy, pleased with her career and her life. She was living in a house on one of the cable car lines with three other professionally employed women, and she felt that she was performing well on her first job and arranging for her next assignment. Then an event occurred that threatened to destroy all her contentment.

> We had received a shipment of thin little wafers from England that had a creme filling flavored with fruit: strawberries and raspberries. They were very good. They were packaged in foil covered boxes, but somehow they had become infested with insects.

We did not think that all of the boxes were infested, because not all of the customers brought them back. But, some people did, and obviously we could not continue to sell them. We couldn't inspect them because there were too many—over $9,000 worth—and because we would have had to tear the foil to open each box. Maria said that the manufacturer would not give us a refund because the infestation doubtless occurred during shipment, or storage at our own warehouse.

Maria told me to get rid of them. I thought that she meant for me to arrange to have them taken to the dump, but she said, "Absolutely not. Call [name of an executive] at [name of a convenience store chain in southern California]. They operate down in the ghetto, and can sell anything. We've got to get our money back. (Statement of Sarah Goodwin)

Exercise. What action would you take if you were Sarah Goodwin?

Portland Machinery Company

Portland Machinery Company is an industrial conglomerate that has grown rapidly through acquisitions. The company has the reputation of taking over other firms, often in depressed industries, and then improving financial performance through strict cost controls and large staff reductions.

My father worked for [name of a company acquired by Portland Machinery] for 32 years. He was a plant manager, in the compressor division. About a week after Portland bought the company, one of their hotshots walked into Dad's office and told him he was through; said his performance had been "unacceptable." I'm just a physician, but I remember enough of freshman economics to know that compressors are an industrial product, and that industrial sales are cyclical. You wait until the bottom of the cycle, and everyone's performance looks bad.

Dad got 11 weeks' severance pay; no pension because he left before he was 60, and no medical insurance. At age 58, Dad is out looking for work, and you know he's not going to be able to find anything. Fortunately, my brother and I can help Mom and Dad, but this has just about destroyed him. He is a decent, hardworking man who devoted his life to a company, and some M.B.A. can come in and say, "Get out."

The really incredible part is that Dad's secretary, who had been with him for over 20 years, began to cry as she watched him start to leave. So they fired her. She doesn't have any children to help her; instead she was supporting her mother.

Then, they got about 40 percent of the staff. Sure, you can build profits if you cut people; the ones who are left will work twice as hard to be able to stay. And if you cut the older people you save lots of money on the pension obligations and medical insurance. But, what a way to do it. Is this what you teach at the business school? (Statement of physician in Ann Arbor)

Fortune Magazine, in 1984, published a study of the impact of mergers and acquisitions upon employees of the acquired firms. It reported that personal tragedies of the sort described above were not uncommon.

Mergers and acquisitions have a human side; a human cost not always figured in when top executives, investment bankers, and take-over lawyers concoct the big deals that are increasingly part of the normal course of business. No statistics show how many employees get relocated, lose jobs, status, benefits, or opportunities, or develop health and family problems. But a good guess is that one-quarter to one-half the employees at the combined organizations are directly affected. *Fortune* estimates that the ten largest of 1983's 1,500 mergers changed the lives of up to 220,000 employees.

* * * * *

Even a merger that results in little change can be unsettling. . . . But the trauma is of a much different order when an acquirer grabs an organization with both hands and shakes.

* * * * *

Cooper Industries, an industrial machinery manufacturer, has a reputation for handling acquisitions roughly. After its 1979 take-over of Gardner-Denver, a maker of mining, drilling, and construction equipment, Cooper shut down the corporate headquarters, decentralized the company, reduced employment in lackluster operations, shrank benefits, and cut working capital. Plenty of human flotsam bobbed in the wake.

* * * * *

Wall Streeters argue that this high human cost was part of the price of making Gardner-Denver healthy. Before Cooper bought it, Gardner-Denver was riddled with operating problems and lacked the management skill to meet the globalized competition of the Seventies. After the takeover, says Goldman Sachs security analyst Thomas G. Burns, "What happened in Gardner-Denver's earning results was really quite handsome." *(Fortune,* July 9, 1984, p. 44f.)

Exercise. What actions would you have taken, were you the executive sent by Portland Machinery Company to take control of the recently acquired compressor division described in the first part of the case? Would you have fired the plant manager, who had 32 years of service with that division?

CHAPTER 2

Managerial Ethics and Microeconomic Theory

We are concerned in this book with ethical dilemmas: decisions and actions faced by managers in which the economic performance and the social performance of the organization are in conflict. These are instances in which someone to whom the organization has some form of obligation—employees, customers, suppliers, distributors, stockholders, or the general population in the area where the company operates—is going to be hurt or harmed in some manner, while the company is going to profit. The question is how to decide: how to find a balance between economic performance and social performance when faced by an ethical dilemma.

A balance is necessary. It is not possible, given the increasingly competitive nature of the business world, always to decide in favor of social performance. It is not possible always to keep in place surplus employees following a merger. It is not possible always to retain obsolete distributors when the economics of the industry have changed. It is not possible always to delay building a dam for power generation because it will destroy recreational opportunities for local residents.

On the other side, however, it is not possible always to decide in favor of economic performance. We can all picture a manager murmuring something about a need to be tough in the three instances above and then firing the surplus employees, replacing the obsolete distributors, and building the new dam. But that was the reason for listing the other ethical dilemmas faced by recent graduates of business schools. Is it possible always to disregard older people, living on fixed incomes, when making a product or pricing decision? Is it possible always to disregard potential customers, and an obligation to be truthful to them, when designing an advertising progam? Is it possible always to disregard unpleasant if not hazardous working conditions for production employees in planning capital improvements at a manufacturing plant? If these illustrations at the operating level are not enough, we can move on to the more dramatic examples at the corporate or strategic level that were listed briefly in the previous chapter. Is it right to bribe foreign political leaders to ensure the purchase of the company's products? Is it right to overbill the Defense Department for large, nonessential expenditures to increase the company's profits? Is it right to make fictitious deposits at banks to earn $8 million of interest? Is it right to offer free vacation trips and cash payments to surgeons to sell nearly $200 million of cataract-replacement lenses?

I think that we can all agree, in some of the instances above, that "No, it is not right." At some point along that vector of examples, listed generally in a ranking of increasing moral severity, people's opinions change from "Yes, that seems to be all right" to "No, that is definitely wrong." It is a question of where to draw the line. It is a question of how to balance the economic versus the social performance of the firm.

There are three forms of analysis that can help in drawing the line, that can assist in reaching a decision on the proper balance between economic and social performance. These forms of analysis are economic, based upon impersonal market forces; legal, based upon impersonal social forces; and philosophical, based upon personal principles and values. In this chapter we are going to look at economic analysis, based upon impersonal market forces.

THE MORAL CONTENT OF MICROECONOMIC THEORY

Economic analysis as a means of finding the proper or moral balance between the economic and social performance of a business firm may seem to you to be an anomaly, an impossibility.

That is not true; there is a definite moral content to microeconomic theory.

For many persons, the concept of morality in microeconomics—the theory of the firm—is a contradiction in terms; they learned the theory as a logical and mathematical approach to markets and prices and production, devoid of moral substance. As a result of this education, most noneconomists, and perhaps a few economists as well, appear to focus almost entirely on profit maximization. They view the theory as descriptive, designed to rationalize the behavior of business managers, and believe that such single-minded pursuit of profit automatically excludes any consideration of environmental health, worker safety, consumer interests, or other "side issues." Overconcentration on profits doubtless has resulted in these and other problems within our society, but that is neither a consequence nor a corollary of microeconomic theory. Microeconomic theory, in its more complete form, addresses these issues and includes ethical as well as economic precepts.

Microeconomic theory in its complete form is more a normative theory of society than a descriptive theory of the firm. Profit maximization is a part of the theory, but it is only a part, and certainly not the central focus—though it must be admitted, and this adds to the lack of understanding, that techniques for profit maximization occupy a central portion of the curriculum at many schools of business administration. The central focus of the larger theory of society is the efficient utilization of resources to satisfy consumer wants and needs. At economic equilibrium—and an essential element in reaching equilibrium throughout the entire economic system is the effort by business managers to balance marginal increases in revenues against marginal increases in costs, which automatically results in optimal profits for the firm within market and resource constraints—it is theoretically possible to achieve Pareto Optimality.

Pareto Optimality refers to a condition in which the scarce resources of society are being used so efficiently by the producing firms, and the goods and services are being distributed so effectively by the competitive markets, that it would be impossible to make any single person better off without harming some other person. Remember this phrase: "It would be impossible to make any single person better off without making some other person worse off." This is the ethical substance of microeconomic theory encapsulated in Pareto Optimality: Produce the maximum economic benefits for society, recognizing the full personal and social costs of that production, and then broaden the receipt of those benefits if necessary by political, not economic, actions.

Pareto Optimality provides the ethical content of microeconomic theory; without this concept of social benefit, the theory deteriorates into a simple prescription for individual gain and corporate profit. With this concept, the theory becomes a means of achieving a social goal: maximum availability of goods and services produced at minimum cost. The theory requires that every business manager attempt to optimize profits. Consequently the decision rule that a microeconomist would propose for finding the proper balance between the economic and social performance of a business firm would be to always be truthful, honorable (i.e., observe contracts), and competitive, and always decide for the greater economic return. The question of this chapter is: Can we use this decision rule when faced with an ethical dilemma?

For many microeconomists, the concept of Pareto Optimality excludes any need to consider ethical dilemmas in management. This view is very direct and can be summarized very simply. "Ethics are not relevant in business, beyond the normal standards not to lie, cheat, or steal. All that is necessary is to maintain price-competitive markets and recognize the full costs of production in those prices, and then the market system will ensure that scarce resources are used to optimally satisfy consumer needs. A firm that is optimally satisfying consumer needs, to the limit of the available resources, is operating most efficiently and most profitably. Consequently, business managers should act to maximize profits, while following legal requirements of noncollusion and equal opportunity and adhering to personal standards of truthfulness and honesty. Profit maximization leads automatically from the satisfaction of individual consumer wants to the generation of maximum social benefits. Profit maximization is the only moral standard needed for management."

Is this summary an overstatement of the microeconomic view of ethics and management? Probably not. The belief that profit maximization leads inexorably to the well-being of society is a central tenet of economic theory and has been stated very succinctly and very clearly by both James McKie of the Brookings Institution and Milton Friedman of the University of Chicago:

> The primary goal and motivating force for business organizations is profit. The firm attempts to make as large a profit as it can, thereby maintaining its efficiency and taking advantage of available opportunities to innovate and contribute to growth. Profits are kept to reasonable or appropriate levels by market competition, which leads the firm pursuing its own self-interest to an end that is not part of its conscious intention: enhancement of the public welfare.[1]

* * * * *

> The view has been gaining widespread acceptance that corporate officials . . . have a "social responsibility" that goes beyond serving the interest of their stockholders or their members. This view shows a fundamental misconception of the character and nature of a free economy. In such an economy, there is one and only one social responsibility of business—to use its resources and engage in activities designed to increase its profits, so long as it stays within the rules of the game, which is to say, engages in open and free competition, without deception or fraud. . . . Few trends could so thoroughly undermine the very foundations of our free society as the acceptance by corporate officials of a social responsibility other than to make as much money for their stockholders as possible.[2]

The statement by Milton Friedman was expanded in an article, "The Social Responsibility of Business Is to Increase Its Profits,"[3] which often is assigned for students at business schools in classes on business economics or business and society. It is a frustrating article to read and then to discuss in class because it never makes clear the theoretical basis of Pareto Optimality; Professor Friedman assumes that the readers recognize and understand that basis of his contention.

THE MORAL PROBLEMS IN MICROECONOMIC THEORY

What is your opinion? Can we accept the microeconomic premise that profit optimization leads directly to maximum social benefits? The response of people trained in other disciplines is often much more pragmatic than theoretical, and it too can be summarized very simply: "Yes, we know the theory, but look at where the blind pursuit of profit has led us: foreign bribes, environmental problems, unsafe products, closed plants, and in-jured workers. We need something more than profit to measure our obligations to society." This view, I think, has been most sen-sibly expressed by Manuel Velasquez of the University of Santa Clara:

> . . . some have argued that in perfectly competitive free markets the pursuit of profit will by itself ensure that the members of soci-ety are served in the most socially beneficial ways. For, in order to be profitable, each firm has to produce only what the members of society want and has to do this by the most efficient means avail-able. The members of society will benefit most, then, if managers do not impose their own values on a business but instead devote themselves to the single-minded pursuit of profit, and thereby de-vote themselves to producing efficiently what the members of soci-ety themselves value.
>
> Arguments of this sort conceal a number of assumptions. . . . First, most industrial markets are not "perfectly competitive" as the argument assumes, and to the extent that firms do not have to compete they can maximize profits in spite of inefficient produc-tion. Second, the argument assumes that any steps taken to in-crease profits will necessarily be socially beneficial, when in fact several ways of increasing profits actually injure society: allowing harmful pollution to go uncontrolled, deceptive advertising, con-cealing product hazards, fraud, bribery, tax evasion, price-fixing, and so on. Third, the argument assumes that by producing what-ever the buying public wants (or values) firms are producing what all the members of society want, when in fact the wants of large segments of society (the poor and the disadvantaged) are not nec-essarily met because they cannot participate fully in the market-place. . . .[4]

This pragmatic response, which can obviously be supported by many examples within our society, is not compelling to most economists. They believe that the issues cited—the lack of com-petitive markets, the presence of injurious practices, and the ex-clusion of some segments of society—are part of economic theory and would be prevented by its strict application. How would they be prevented? Here, it is necessary to provide an explanation of the extensive structure of economic theory and of the logical interrelationships that exist among the components in that structure: the individual consumers, product markets, produc-ing firms, factor markets, factor owners, and public institutions. (The "factors" are the scarce resources of labor, capital, and material used in the production of goods and services.) Doubtless an explanation of this structure and these interrelationships will be dull for those with a good grasp of microeconomic theory, and trying for all others, but this explanation is necessary to deal with the ethical problems in the theory on a meaningful basis. If you truly are bored with microeconomic theory and willing to accept the rationality of the structure, skip ahead to page 46 and dive directly into the ethical claims of the theory.

THE BASIC STRUCTURE OF MICROECONOMIC THEORY

Microeconomic theory is complex. Perhaps, to make this brief explanation more comprehensible, it would be well to start with an overall summary. The focus of the theory, as stated previously, is the efficient utilization of scarce resources to maximize the production of wanted goods and services. The mechanism of the theory is the market structure: each firm is located between a "factor" market for the input factors of production (labor, material, and capital) and a "product" market for the output goods and services. The demand for each good or service is aggregated from the preference functions of individual consumers, who act to maximize their satisfactions from a limited mix of products. The supply of each good or service is aggregated from the production schedules of individual firms, which act to balance their marginal revenues and marginal costs at a limited level of capacity. The production of goods and services creates derived demands for the input factors of labor, material, and capital. These factors are substitutable—can be interchanged—so the derived demands vary with the costs. These costs, of course, reflect the constrained supplies in the different factor markets. A firm attempting to minimize costs and maximize revenues will therefore use the most available resources to produce the most needed products, generating not only the greatest profits for itself but the greatest benefits for society. The components of the theory, and the relationships among these components, which together produce corporate profits and social benefits, may be more understandable in graphic form, as shown in Figure 2–1.

Now it is necessary to work through the theory in somewhat greater detail to indicate the inclusion of ethical concepts and to be able to discuss the ethical problems that are integral with it.

FIGURE 2–1
Graphic Summary of Microeconomic Theory

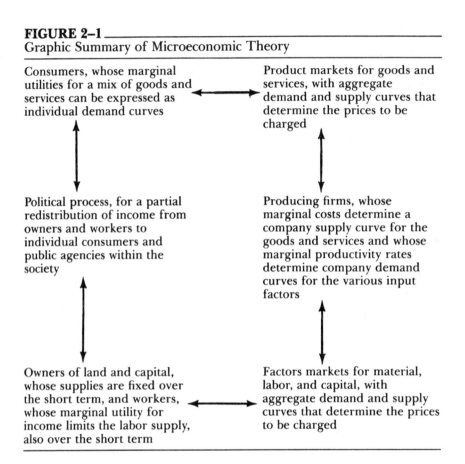

Consumers, whose marginal utilities for a mix of goods and services can be expressed as individual demand curves

Product markets for goods and services, with aggregate demand and supply curves that determine the prices to be charged

Political process, for a partial redistribution of income from owners and workers to individual consumers and public agencies within the society

Producing firms, whose marginal costs determine a company supply curve for the goods and services and whose marginal productivity rates determine company demand curves for the various input factors

Owners of land and capital, whose supplies are fixed over the short term, and workers, whose marginal utility for income limits the labor supply, also over the short term

Factors markets for material, labor, and capital, with aggregate demand and supply curves that determine the prices to be charged

Individual Consumers

Each consumer has a slightly different set of preferences for the various goods and services that are available, and these preferences can be expressed as "utilities," or quantitative measures of the usefulness of a given product or service to a specific customer. The "marginal utility," or extra usefulness, of one additional unit of that product or service to that customer tends to decline, for eventually the person will have a surfeit of the good. The price that the person is willing to pay for the good also declines along with marginal utility or degree of surfeit. Price relative to the number of units that will be purchased by a given person at a given time forms the individual demand curve (see Figure 2–2).

FIGURE 2–2
Consumer Demand Curve

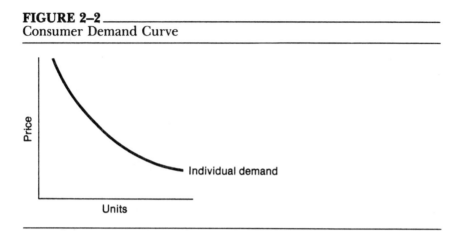

Price can also be used to compare the relative usefulness of different goods and services to an individual. It can be expected that a person selecting a mix of products will choose an assortment of goods and services such that marginal utility per monetary unit would be equal for all the items at a given level of spending for this individual. Each good would be demanded up to the point where the marginal utility per dollar would be exactly the same as the marginal utility per dollar for any other good. If a customer had a higher marginal utility relative to price for any particular good, he or she would doubtless substitute more of that good for some of the others to achieve a better balance among his or her preferences. The final balance or mix, where the marginal utilities per monetary unit are equal for all products and services, can be termed the point of equilibrium for that customer.

The concept of consumer equilibrium is an important element in the structure of the economic condition termed Pareto Optimality. A customer with balanced marginal utilities per monetary unit for all available goods and services cannot be made better off at his or her level of spending, according to his or her standards of preference. The customer may buy hamburgers, french fries, and beer, and we may think that he or she should be buying fish, fresh vegetables, and fruit, but that person is satisfying his or her standards, not our own, and they are being satisfied up to the limits of his or her ceiling on expenditures. Consequently, that person cannot be made better off without an increase in disposable income. Now, let us look at the determination of the level of disposable income in microeconomic theory. This is more complex than the determination of the mix of desired purchases, but the logical structure can be followed through the product markets, the producing firms, the factor markets, the private owners of those factors, and the public processes for redistribution of factor income.

Product Markets

A product market consists of all the customers for a given good or service, together with all the producing firms that supply that good or service. The individual demand curves of all the customers can be aggregated to form a market demand curve. The market demand curve reflects the total demand for a good or service, relative to price, and it generally slopes downward, indicating increased potential purchases at the lower price levels. Crossing this market demand curve is a market supply curve that portrays the total available supply, again relative to price. The market supply curve generally slopes upward, for the higher the price, the more units in total most companies can be expected to manufacture, until they reach a short-term limit of capacity. The market price, of course, is set at the intersection of the curves representing aggregate demand and aggregate supply (see Figure 2–3).

Producing Firms

The aggregate supply curve, the "other half" of each product market, is formed by adding together the individual supply curves of all the producers. These individual supply curves are generated by the cost structures of the producing firms at different levels of production, while the actual level of production is determined by a comparison of "marginal revenues" and "marginal costs." The marginal revenue of a producing firm is the extra revenue that the firm would receive by selling one additional unit of the good or service. To sell that additional unit in a fully price-competitive market, it is necessary to move down the aggregate demand curve to a slightly lower price level. To sell that additional unit in a non-price-competitive market, it is necessary to spend greater amounts on advertising and promo-

FIGURE 2–3
Market Demand and Supply Curve

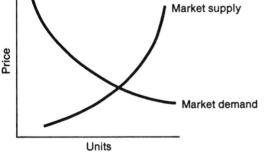

tion to differentiate the product from those manufactured by other firms. Under either alternative, the marginal revenue from selling the last unit will be less than the average revenue from selling all other units; marginal revenues inevitably decrease with volume.

The marginal cost of the producing firm is the obverse of the marginal revenue. Marginal cost is the extra expense that the firm would incur by producing one additional unit of the product or service. Marginal costs initially decline with volume due to economies of scale and learning curve effects, but they eventually rise due to diminishing returns as the physical capacity of the plant is approached. The rising portion of the marginal cost curve forms the supply curve of the firm; it represents the number of units that the firm should produce and supply to the market at each price level (see Figure 2–4).

The producing firm achieves equilibrium when marginal costs are equal to marginal revenues. At the intersection of the marginal cost and marginal revenue curves, the profits of the firm are maximized. The firm can increase profits only by improving its technology; this would change the marginal costs and consequently the supply curve. However, over the long term, all firms would adopt the new technology and achieve the same cost structure. Production equilibrium would be reestablished at the new intersections of the marginal cost and marginal revenue curves for all firms within the industry.

FIGURE 2–4
Marginal Cost Curve

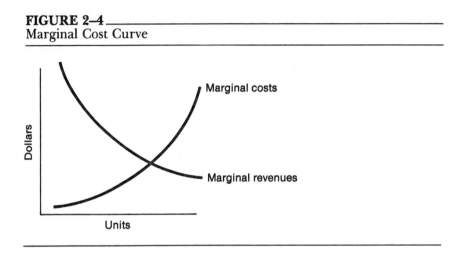

All the costs of production have to be included in computing the marginal cost curve for a firm. This is the second of the ethical constructs in microeconomic theory, along with the individual selection of goods and services according to private preference standards, or "utilities." The internal personal costs (e.g., hazardous working conditions) and the external social costs (e.g., harmful environmental discharges) have to be computed, so that customers pay the full costs of production. The technology, of course, can be changed to improve working conditions and reduce environmental discharges, and this should be done to bring marginal costs down to marginal revenues at a new, nonhazardous and nonpolluting equilibrium, but it is an essential element in microeconomic theory that product-market prices reflect the *full* costs of production.

Factor Markets

The technology of the producing firm determines the maximum output of goods and services that can be achieved for a given mix of input factors. The input factors of production are land (an apparently obsolete term that instead refers to all of the basic raw materials), labor, and capital. Charges for the input factors are rents for the land and other basic resources, wages for the labor, and interest for the capital. These charges are interdependent because the factors are interrelated; that is, one factor may be substituted for others in the production function. The relationships among these input factors, and the amount of one that would have to be used to substitute for another, are determined by the technology of the production function and by the "marginal productivity" of each factor for a given technology. The marginal productivity of a factor of production is the additional output generated by adding one more unit of that factor while keeping all others constant. For example, it is possible to add one additional worker to a production line without changing the capital investments in the line and the material components of the product; there should be an increase in the physical output of that production line, and that increase, measured in units or portions of units, would be the marginal productivity of that worker. To maximize profits, a company should increase the use of each factor of production until the value of its marginal product (the increase in unit output, or productivity, times the value of those units) equals the cost of the input factor.

Factor Owners

The aggregate demand for each factor of production is equal to the proportion of that factor used in the production function of each firm times the output of those functions supplied to meet the product market demand. The demand for each factor of production is therefore "derived" from the primary markets for goods and services. The aggregate supply of each factor of production is limited. Over the long term, stocks of the basic materials may be expanded by bringing into production marginal agricultural lands, oilfields, and ore mines, and the reserves of investment capital may be increased by raising the rate of capital formation. Over the short term, however, the supply amounts are fixed. Aggregate supplies of labor are also limited, though for a different cause: each worker has a marginal utility for income that decreases and becomes negative as his or her desire for greater leisure exceeds his or her preference for further work. This negative utility function creates a "backward sloping" supply curve for labor and sharply limits the amounts available at the higher wage rates. The price system in the different factor markets, therefore, ensures that the limited factors of production will be used in the most economically effective manner to produce the goods and services to be sold in the product markets, and that the rents, wages, and interest paid for these factors

FIGURE 2–5
Factor Supply Curves

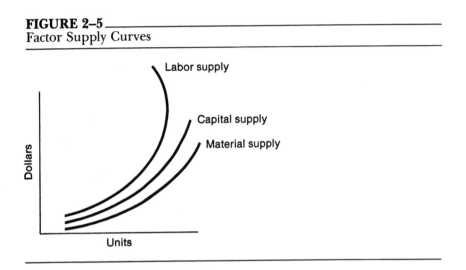

will reflect both the productivity of the factor and the derived demand of the goods (see Figure 2–5).

Political Processes

The owners of the factors of production, within a capitalistic society, are also the customers for the products and services generated by the production functions at the various firms. The owners receive the rents, the wages, and the interest payments for the use of their resources and then purchase the goods and services they want, following their personal preferences or utilities. There is a political process for the redistribution of the rents, wages, and interest payments, through both tax provisions and welfare allocations, so that no individual or group is unable to participate in the product markets for the various goods and services. This political process is the third ethical construct in microeconomic theory; it ensures that the distribution of the revenues for material, capital, and labor will be "equitable," following a democratically determined definition of equity.

THE MORAL CLAIMS OF MICROECONOMIC THEORY

Now that there is a common understanding of the basic structure of microeconomic theory, or the logical system of relationships among individual customers, product markets, producing firms, factor markets, resource owners, and political processes, it is possible to look at the claims of that theory relative to the social welfare. There are five explicit assertions:

1. The price mechanisms of the factor markets allocate the scarce resources of society to their most effective uses. The marginal productivity of each factor together with the cost (reflecting supply versus demand) determines the relative usage of the factors by the producing firms. At factor equilibrium, it would be impossible to expand total production without an increase in resource supply.

2. The production functions of the producing firms convert the limited input factors into wanted output goods and services by the most effective methods (process technologies) and at the most efficient rates (output amounts). A firm's technology and capacity are long-term decisions, while the operating rate is a short-term choice, but all are based upon the balance between marginal revenues and marginal costs. Internal personal harms and external social damages are included in the marginal costs. At process equilibrium, it would be impossible to convert resources into products more efficiently and with less personal harm or social damage without an advance in technology.

3. The price mechanisms of the product markets distribute the wanted goods and services of society to their most effective uses. The marginal utilities of each customer together with the prices (again reflecting supply versus demand) for the various products determine the relative consumption of the goods and services. At market equilibrium, it would be impossible to improve consumer satisfaction without an increase in personal income.

4. The political processes of the national society determine the personal income of each consumer through democratic means. The income may be distributed according to ownership of the factors of production, or according to an individual's need, effort, contribution, or competence. Distribution of the benefits of the economic system is a political, not an economic, process.

5. The economic system, provided the managers of the producing firms act to maximize profits, the customers for the goods and services act to maximize satisfactions, and the owners of the resources act to maximize revenues, the economic system will operate efficiently, producing the greatest output of wanted goods and services for the least input of scarce labor, capital, and material. If the revenues to the owners of the factors of production are equitably redistributed to the customers of the producing firms through a democratic decision process, it would be impossible to improve the life of any member of the system without harming the life of another member, because the system would have reached Pareto Optimality. Consequently, the social responsibility of the managers of the producing firms is to maximize profits and leave the redistribution of economic benefits to the political process.

PRAGMATIC OBJECTIONS TO MICROECONOMIC THEORY

The usual objections to microeconomic theory are pragmatic in nature, based upon very obvious problems in our national society, and they generally include the three issues discussed by Professor Velasquez in the statement quoted earlier in this chapter:

1. *The exclusion of segments of society.* It is alleged that the minorities and the poor, because they lack ownership of any of the factors of production beyond their unskilled labor, receive inadequate income to participate in the product markets and consequently cannot maximize their own satisfactions in any meaningful way. The microeconomic response is quite obvious. "We grant you that this happens, but it is the fault of the political process and not of the economic system. You develop logically attractive political decision rules for the more equitable division of the benefits, and we will work to economically maximize the production of those benefits within market and resource constraints."

2. *The presence of injurious practices.* It is also alleged that managers of productive firms, because of an excessive concern with maximizing profits, have permitted or even encouraged some practices that are injurious to some members of society, through workplace dangers or environmental pollution, or that are destructive to the market system, through purchase bribes or employment discrimination. Here, the response of most economists would be that these problems occur, but that they would not occur under the strict application of the theory. Let us look at a number of specific problems and the theoretical solutions:

Purchase Bribes. Personal payments to influence purchase decisions are evidently common overseas, and not unknown within the United States. In an efficient market, however, bribes would be futile; they would raise the cost function by an amount equivalent to the payment, so that nonbribing competitors would have an obvious price advantage. The microeconomic response is obvious: Insist that purchase decisions be open and subject to public comparison of the bids, to ensure the selection of the lowest-priced proposal to supply needed goods and services. The lowest-priced proposal would necessarily come from a nonbribing competitor.

Process Pollutants. Many industrial processes result in toxic residues and inert materials as by-products, which are now either discharged as air or water pollutants or buried as liquid or solid wastes. The toxic by-products have an obvious social cost, both immediate and long term. The microeconomic response has been clearly stated many times: companies should recognize these costs that are external to the productive process and include them in the pricing function. It might be expected, were these external costs accurately computed, that investments in proper disposal equipment would become clearly beneficial for the firm, or if they were fully included in the price, the product would become overly expensive for the customer; under either alternative, the amount of pollution would be substantially reduced.

Workplace Hazards. It would appear that many of the mechanical hazards of industrial processing have been eliminated; 40 years of state and federal labor laws have removed the unprotected belts, open gearing, and nonshielded presses. Chemical risks still remain, however, and psychological problems will probably always be a part of mass manufacturing, due to the repetitive nature of the tasks and the time constraints of the process. The microeconomic response to workplace hazards is similar to that for process pollutants: the nonfactor costs of production should be computed and added to the price. Certainly, if the market is to operate efficiently to allocate resources within the society, customers have to pay the full costs of production, not partial costs subsidized by the physical or mental health of the workers.

Product Dangers. The press has recently reported numerous instances of unsafe products, particularly in the automobile industry. Gas tanks poorly located, radial tires poorly fabricated, and automatic transmissions poorly designed have all been mentioned, together with such nonautomotive products as hair dryers (containing asbestos), teddy bears (containing sharp objects), and packaged foods (containing nonnutrients). I think it safe to assume· that the microeconomic response would be that a product offered for sale within a competitive market should perform the function for which it was designed, and that many of the reported failures and hazards come from decisions to differentiate products in slight or artificial ways to avoid the discipline of price competition. Whatever the cause of product failure and hazards, the costs of improper design are now being charged back against the manufacturing firms through liability suits and jury awards, and it can be assumed that product safety will soon be improved as a result of objective economic analysis.

Minority Employment. Racial or sexual discrimination in employment, in an efficient labor market, would be self-defeating; a work force limited to young or middle-aged white males would raise the cost of labor in the productive function and provide the nondiscriminating employer with a cost advantage. It is assumed, in economic analysis, that all groups are equal in performance capabilities. Training might be needed to justify that assumption, but the microeconomic response would be that training to correct social injustices should be provided as a public investment. Cost-benefit analysis would assuredly show an economic return on that investment, as well as a social gain.

3. *The absence of competitive markets.* Lastly, it is often claimed that the product markets for consumer goods and services are not price competitive because of oligopolistic practices among the producing firms serving those markets. Companies have become much larger recently, doubtless due to economies of scale in production and distribution, while products have become more "differentiated," marked by only slight or imagined distinctions in performance and design but supported by excessive advertising. The dominance of large firms in each market, and the inability of customers to judge the relative worth of products in those markets, is said to lead toward "administered" rather than competitive prices. Administered pricing, where the price level is set by the company to provide a set return above costs without reference to either supply or demand, of course destroys the efficiency of the market. The economic response, however, is very simple. "Oh, we grant you that market structures are not truly competitive, and that market processes are not actually efficient under current conditions. However, no one is advocating limited competition or inadequate information. Public policy changes to restrict competitor size and to ensure consumer information are needed to reestablish the discipline of the market."

THEORETIC OBJECTIONS TO MICROECONOMIC THEORY

Microeconomic theory is awesomely complete. There are few operating decisions in business to which it could not be applied—from hiring workers, purchasing supplies, and borrowing money to selecting technologies, establishing capacities, and setting prices. Likewise, there are few ethical problems to which microeconomic theory is not applicable, whether purchase bribes, process pollutants, workplace hazards, product dangers, or racial discrimination. It is very difficult to say, "Here is a managerial decision or action with definite ethical implications that is not included in the theory."

Microeconomic theory is also enviably unified. All the managerial decisions and actions work together, through a system of explicit relationships, to create a socially desirable goal: maximum output of the wanted goods and services at a minimum input of the scarce material, capital, and labor. It is very difficult to say, "Here is a managerial decision or action following microeconomic theory that does not lead to a socially beneficial outcome."

Where does this discussion lead us? Are we forced to accept microeconomic theory as an ethical system of belief for business management because of the complete and unified nature of the paradigm? Should we always act to maximize profits, as long as we are truthful, honest, and competitive, and use the concept of Pareto Optimality as the substitute for our ethical concerns? Or, is there a theoretic problem with that paradigm? Most noneconomists are intuitively distressed by the proposal that business managers have no moral responsibilities to other members of society, outside of fiduciary duties to a small circle of owners, and that managers also are governed by no moral requirements of behavior beyond adhering to personal standards of honesty and truthfulness, observing legal statutes for contracts and against collusion, and computing accurate costs for personal harms and social dangers. Why is this distressing, and what are the arguments against the microeconomic model that can be expressed on a theoretic rather than a pragmatic or intuitive basis? There are two major arguments; one pertains to the assumptions about human nature and the second centers on the assumptions about human worth that are part of microeconomic theory.

1. *Assumptions about the nature of human beings.* The microeconomic model is utilitarian (see Chapter 4 for a definition of utilitarianism, a philosophic system that has often been roughly translated as "the greatest good for the greatest number"). It takes the position that the ultimate end is the greatest general good, and it defines that good as the maximum benefits of consumer products and services at the minimum costs of labor, capital, and material. The problem, as with all utilitarian theories, is that the distribution of the benefits and the imposition of the costs may be unjust. Consequently, it is necessary to add a political process to the economic paradigm to ensure justice in the distribution of benefits and the imposition of costs. But, "justice" is defined in the theory as a democratically determined pattern of distribution and imposition; this pattern does not follow a rule such as, to each person equally, or to each according to his or her need, to his or her effort, to his or her contribution, to his or her competence, or even to his or her ownership of the factors of production. Instead, the pattern varies with the collective opinions of the members of society. This requires all members of society to be actively concerned with the charitable distribution of social benefits and imposition of social costs at the same time as they are actively concerned with the personal maximization of material goods and services in the product markets and of financial wages, rents, and interest payments in the factor markets, solely for themselves. I think that we can safely say that human nature exhibits both selfish and generous traits, and we can doubtless go further and accept that human beings can perform selfish and then generous acts alternately, but it would seem an extreme assumption to believe that people can concurrently be generously attentive to others in all political decisions and selfishly attentive to themselves in all economic activities, and never confuse the two roles. The microeconomic model would appear to be based upon an exceedingly complex and unlikely view of the *nature* of human beings.

2. *Assumptions about the value of human beings.* The microeconomic model is impersonal, for it requires that everyone be treated as a means to an end and not as an end in himself or herself. Customers for goods and services are people who maximize material satisfactions as a means of determining product-demand curves. Owners of land, capital, and labor are people who maximize financial revenues as a means of determining factor-supply curves. Company managers are people who maximize corporate profits as a means of balancing market demand and factor supply. No one acts as an individual human being, pursuing personal goals worthy of consideration and respect. This denial of worth can be seen particularly clearly in the position of the manager of the firm, who must act solely as an agent for the financial interests of the stockholders. What does this do to self-esteem and to self-respect? How can people live worthwhile lives when always being treated as a means to other people's ends— or, perhaps even worse, when always treating others as means to their own ends—even though the society as an economic system may have achieved Pareto Optimality? The microeconomic model would appear to be based upon an exceedingly low view of the *worth* of human beings.

Where does this discussion of managerial ethics and microeconomic theory lead us? There would seem to be two major conclusions. If we look at microeconomic theory as a structured pattern of relationships explaining the optimal uses of scarce material, capital, and labor to produce the optimal numbers of consumer goods and services, then it is a logically complete and intellectually satisfying view of the world. But, if we look at microeconomic theory as an ethical system of belief, explaining our responsibility to others within the company and within the society—to employees, customers, suppliers, distributors, and residents of the local area—then it simply falls apart because of the unlikely assumptions about human nature and human worth. We are going to have to look elsewhere for a means of reaching decisions when confronted with an ethical dilemma, with a conflict between the economic performance and the social performance of a business firm. We are going to have to look either to the rule of law or to the doctrines of normative philosophy to determine what is "right" and "just" and "proper."

Footnotes

1. James McKie, "Changing Views," *Social Responsibility and the Business Predicament* (Washington, D.C.: Brookings Institution, 1974), p. 19.
2. Milton Friedman, *Capitalism and Freedom* (Chicago: University of Chicago Press, 1962), p. 133.
3. *New York Times Magazine*, September 13, 1970, p. 32f.
4. Manuel Velasquez, *Business Ethics: Concepts and Causes* (New York: Prentice-Hall, 1982), pp. 17–18.

CASES

Financial Compensation for the Victims at Bhopal

On December 3, 1984, some 2,000 people were killed and 200,000 were injured when a cloud of poisonous methyl isocyanate gas was accidentally released from the Union Carbide Company plant in Bhopal, India. The methyl isocyanate was used to manufacture Sevin, a plant pesticide that was distributed widely throughout India for use on that country's corn, rice, soybean, cotton, and alfalfa crops. It was said that the use of Sevin increased the harvest of the food crops by over 10 percent, enough to feed 70 million people.

The accident apparently occurred when between 120 and 240 gallons of water were introduced into a tank containing 90,000 pounds of methyl isocyanate.[1] The tank also contained approximately 3,000 pounds of chloroform, used as a solvent in the manufacture of methyl isocyanate; the two chemicals should have been separated before storage but had not been for some time in the operating process at Bhopal.

The water reacted exothermically (producing heat) with the chloroform, generating chlorine ions, which led to corrosion of the tank walls, and the iron oxide from the corrosion in turn reacted exothermically with the methyl isocyanate. The increase in heat and pressure was rapid but unnoticed, because the pressure gauge on the tank had been inoperable for four months and the operators in the control room, monitoring a remote temperature gauge, were accustomed to higher-than-specified heat levels (25°C. rather than the 0°C. in the operating instructions) due to the continual presence of the chloroform and some water vapor in the tank. The refrigeration unit built to cool the storage tank had been disconnected six months previously. The "scrubber," a safety device to neutralize the methyl isocyanate with caustic soda, had been under repair since June. An operator, alarmed by the suddenly increasing temperature, attempted to cool the tank by spraying it with water, but by then the reaction was unstoppable, at a probable 200°C. The rupture disc (a steel plate in the line, to prevent accidental operation of the safety valve) broke, the safety valve opened (just before, it is assumed, the tank would have burst), and over half the 45 tons of methyl isocyanate in storage were discharged into the air.

Following the accident, Union Carbide officials in the United States denied strongly that their firm was responsible for the tragedy. They made the following three statements in support of that position:

1. The Bhopal plant was 50.9 percent owned by the American firm, but the parent corporation had been able to exercise little control. All managerial and technical personnel were citizens of India at the insistence of the Indian government. No Americans were permanently employed at the plant. Safety warnings from visiting American inspectors about the Sevin-manufacturing process had been ignored.

2. Five automatic safety devices that had originally been installed as part of the Sevin-manufacturing process had, by the time of the accident, been either removed and replaced by manual safety methods, allegedly to increase employment, shut down for repair, or disconnected as part of a cost-reduction program. Automatic temperature and pressure warning signals had been removed soon after construction. The repairs on the automatic scrubber unit had extended over six months. The refrigeration unit had not been used to cool the tank and had been inoperable for over a year.

3. The Bhopal plant had been built in partnership with the Indian government to increase employment in that country. Union Carbide would have preferred to make Sevin in the United States and ship it to India for distribution and sale, because the insecticide could be made less expensively in the United States due to substantial economies of scale in the manufacturing process.

Warren Anderson, chairman of Union Carbide, stated that while he believed that the American company was not legally liable for the tragedy due to the three points above, it was still "morally" responsible, and he suggested that the firm should pay prompt financial compensation to those killed and injured in the accident.

Exercise. Assume that the question of legal liability for the accident at Bhopal never will be settled, due to differences in the law between the two countries and the difficulties of establishing jurisdiction. Assume, however, that the American company is morally responsible for the tragedy, as admitted by the chairman, because it was the majority owner and yet did not insist that the unsafe process be shut down. What factors would you consider in setting "just" financial compensation for each of the victims?

Footnote

1. Seven engineers and scientists from the Union Carbide Corporation were sent to Bhopal to assist in the safe disposal of the remaining methyl isocyanate at that site and to investigate the reasons for the accident. They were not permitted to interview operators of the Sevin process nor to inspect the methyl isocyanate storage tank and related piping. They were permitted

to obtain samples of the residues from the nearly ruptured tank; through experimentation they were able to replicate reactions that led to residues with the same chemical properties in the same proportions. The account, therefore, is a hypothesis for the tragedy, not a proven series of events.

Greenmail Payments and Takeover Fees

"Greenmail" refers to the payments made to selected stockholders in order for a company to repurchase some of the large blocks of stock that had been accumulated during a corporate takeover attempt. The stock is generally purchased at a premium, above the market, and the payment of this premium represents a loss to the other stockholders.

> Potlatch Corp. bought back a 7.1% stake from the Belzberg family of Canada, settling a takeover threat but further depressing the stock price, which already is irking continuing holders.
> Potlatch, a San Francisco-based forest products company, said it paid $43 each, or about $46.7 million, for the roughly 1.1 million common shares held by the Belzbergs. . . .
> Potlatch's stock dropped on news of the agreement. In New York Stock Exchange composite trading yesterday, Potlatch shares closed at $38.25, down $1.50. . . . With the buyback from the Belzbergs, plus additional purchases made to thwart the family's efforts, Potlatch now has about 13 million shares outstanding. The figures indicate paper losses to continuing holders of nearly $70 million.[1]

"Takeover fees" are the payments made to law firms and investment bankers during a takeover attempt; they tend to be large, particularly when considered in comparison to the expense cuts and work force reductions that frequently take place following the merger.

> Last Saturday night, Pantry Pride Inc. Chairman Ronald O. Perelman entertained 30 aides, lawyers and investment bankers at the exclusive East Side nightspot Le Club. The occasion was a victory party to celebrate winning the takeover fight for Revlon Inc., complete with tablecloths, said one guest, done in "Revlon lipstick red."
> In fact, both Revlon and Pantry Pride advisers had plenty to be happy about. Investment bankers and lawyers are likely to rake in $100 million or more in fees from the bitter, nearly three-month

takeover battle for Revlon, the participants say. That would make Revlon the biggest bonanza ever in Wall Street's booming takeover game. "It's the deal of the century," crows one investment banker.

*　*　*　*　*

Wall Street sources say the biggest winner in the battle for Revlon is Pantry Pride's investment banker, Drexel Burnham Lambert, Inc. It will get an estimated $60 million in fees for services that include raising $1.5 billion for the hostile takeover through the sale of high-yield low-rated "junk bonds."

Another Pantry Pride adviser, Morgan Stanley & Co., will get as much as $30 million for its role, which includes finding buyers for different pieces of Revlon, a New York–based beauty products and health care company that now will be broken up by Mr. Perelman.

And Lazard Freres & Co., Revlon's investment banker, will get $11 million.[2]

Exercise. Greenmail and takeover fees are not ethical dilemmas in the accepted sense of a conflict between the economic performance and the social performance of an organization, but they do represent very large payments made to very selected groups of people. Are they, in your opinion, "right" and "just" and "proper"?

Footnotes

1. *The Wall Street Journal,* Nov. 13, 1985, p. 5.
2. *The Wall Street Journal,* Nov. 8, 1985, p. 6.

AMF Corporation and Pension Fund Reversion

AMF Corporation (originally American Machine and Foundry) is a large conglomerate that focuses primarily on leisure products. The company makes Hatteras motor yachts, Alcort sailboats, Tyrolia ski bindings, Head skis and tennis rackets, AMF automatic pinspotters and bowling supplies, Ben Hogan golf clubs, etc. They also manufacture some industrial products such as electronic controls, relay switches, and circuit breakers, and they distribute food service products to restaurants. The company was severely affected by the recession that started in 1978, and earnings declined sharply from 1980 to 1983.

EXHIBIT 1
Sales Revenues and Aftertax Profits of AMF Corporation, 1980–1983 (000s omitted).

	1980	1981	1982	1983
Sales revenues	1,015,483	1,115,376	1,018,625	935,693
Aftertax profits	58,016	29,946	12,271	(3,241)

SOURCE: Company annual reports

In 1984, it was felt that aftertax income and depreciation from ongoing operations were not providing adequate cash to finance new products. The sale of equity would have been difficult, due to a low stock price, and banks were hesitant to make further loans. There was, however, within the company a ready source of additional cash: the employee pension fund which was "overfunded" by nearly $100 million.

Employee pension funds may be of two types: defined benefit and defined contribution. In a defined contribution plan, the company makes a monthly payment to the pension fund, generally at a certain percentage of the employee's salary or wages; these funds are invested, and at retirement the employee receives the money that was contributed in his or her name, plus the recorded earnings. Instead of a lump-sum payment, it is much more common to use the same amount of money to purchase an annuity, which provides a monthly income for the person over his or her lifetime. There have been no "reversions" with defined contribution plans because the funds legally belong to the employees.

In a defined benefit plan, the employee is guaranteed a set amount upon retirement, and the company makes contributions to the pension fund at a rate that has been actuarially determined to meet that amount. The actuarial rate is usually determined assuming a given return on pension fund investments, often 8.0 percent or 8.5 percent. Due to the stock market expansion from 1980 to 1983, however, and the high interest rates that were available on bond and mortgage investments, the earnings at many pension funds rose substantially above 8.0 percent or 8.5 percent. At AMF, the return averaged 16.7 percent per year for more than seven years.[1] The amount of money that was felt to be "overfunded"—above the amount needed to meet the defined benefits—was more than $100 million.

In 1985, AMF terminated the existing pension plan, purchased annuities to meet the defined benefits due to all employees, and "reverted" the $100 million for investment in the company. AMF was not the first firm to have done this; it was reported that more than 300 companies had replaced their defined-benefit pension plans with purchased employee annuities, claiming over $3 billion in reversions. Opinions of people affected by these actions differed widely:

> "If benefits are secure," assures Sylvester J. Schieber, director of research and information at Wyatt Co., a consultant and actuary, "then the employer is meeting his requirements."[2]

* * * * *

AMF had either some bad luck or some bad management. They sold their Head sportswear and their Harley-Davidson motorcycle divisions just before both products became popular. They got out of lawn and garden tractors and lawnmowers, which comprised their wheeled-products division, just as the recession was coming to an end and people started buying again. Then they got into the oilfield service business just as energy prices started to fall. They're using the pension fund money to make up for their own mistakes. (Statement of industry analyst)

* * * * *

Congratulations on "AMF's agony over tapping the pension till" (Corporate Finance, Jan. 21) though you might have said "raiding" instead of "tapping." The $100 million taken from the pension fund is the result not of superior management but of inflation— the same inflation that has made the pensions of those who retired 10, 15 or 20 years ago practically worthless today. Just as Social Security has indexed pensions to offset inflation, most companies with any self-respect have periodically used a portion of such profits to increase the benefits to their retirees. But not AMF. About 10 years ago it increased benefits for those who had retired by about 5 percent, and that's it. The pensions of those who retired from AMF 10 to 15 years ago are now worth considerably less than half of what they were on retirement—and now AMF has taken every penny of the fund's earnings that could have brought them some relief.[3]

Exercise. What, in your opinion, should AMF have done with the "surplus" finds in the employee pension fund?

Footnotes

1. *Business Week,* January 21, 1985, p. 97.
2. Ibid.
3. Letters to the Editor, *Business Week,* February 4, 1985, p. 8.

CHAPTER 3

Managerial Ethics and the Rule of Law

In this chapter, we will look at the law as a possible basis for managerial decision when one is confronted with an ethical dilemma. The law is a set of rules, established by society, to govern behavior within that society. Why not, then, fall back upon those rules when faced with a conflict between the economic performance of an organization and the social performance of that organization? Why not let the law decide, particularly in a democratic society where the argument can easily be made that the rules within the law represent the collective moral judgments made by members of the society? Why not follow these collective oral judgments, instead of trying to establish our individual moral opinions?

There are numerous examples of laws that do reflect collective moral judgments. Almost everybody within the United States would agree that unprovoked assault is wrong; we have laws against assault. Almost everybody would agree that toxic chemical discharges are wrong; we have laws against pollution. Almost all of us would agree that charitable giving is right; we have no laws against charitable giving. Instead we have laws—provisions within the tax code—that encourage gifts of money, food, and clothing to the poor, and to organizations that work to assist the poor. The question of this chapter is whether we can use this set of rules—often complex, occasionally obsolete, and continually changing—to form "just" and "proper" and "right" decisions when faced with a choice between our economic gain and our social obligations.

Let me give an illustration of the use of law to justify a decision in an ethical dilemma. The example is a situation that bankers face nearly every day: that between investing in a new, small company that will provide the local community with more job opportunities and higher tax payments to support schools and other needed social services, or loaning the same funds to an established, larger company operating in a distant city. The risk is obviously greater for the first investment, but banks are forbidden by law from charging usurious (too high, or excessive) interest rates to compensate for the risk.

How would you decide in that instance? It is possible, of course, to fall back upon the market and say that the law prohibiting usurious interest rates should be repealed, so that all companies would pay the true costs of their borrowings. Capital is one of the factors of production, along with labor and materials, and the microeconomic argument is that companies should pay prices determined by the factor markets. In this instance, the argument would be that the small, local company should pay the interest rate demanded by a free, efficient, and effective market for loans; if the small local company were unable to pay this risk-adjusted rate, then the money should be invested elsewhere, at the next highest risk-adjusted rate that could be paid, in order to maximize the production of needed goods and services at minimal costs in the use of resources. As was seen in Chapter 2, there are both practical and theoretical problems with this view. The three practical problems are rather basic:

1. Few factor markets, except those for widely available commodities, are truly free in that most tend to be dominated by large corporations and wealthy individuals who determine rather than respond to prices.
2. Few factor markets, again except those for the commodities, are truly efficient in that the full range of price-risk and cost-volume alternatives is not generally known by all participants.
3. Few factor markets—and this is particularly true of the market for capital—are completely effective, because it is difficult to compute the precise risks and accurate costs

for different companies in different industries at different times.

The microeconomic response to these three pragmatic problems is that society should add a political process to regulate some prices and allocate some resources, outside of the market process. This proposal, as was also seen in the last chapter, immediately encounters the objection that it requires people to be generously attentive to other people in all political decisions and selfishly attentive only to themselves in all economic activities, and never confuse the two roles. This, it was concluded, is an exceedingly complex and unlikely view of the nature of human beings.

LAW AS A GUIDE TO MORAL CHOICE

We cannot rely upon the market as a guide for managerial decisions and actions when faced with an ethical dilemma, but how about the law? The legal argument is very different. The legal argument is that society has established a set of rules, and that these rules reflect the collective choices of members of society regarding any decisions and actions that affect the welfare of society. This argument can be applied to the particular instance of a bank officer forced to make up his or her mind between a high-risk loan to a small, local company with the return—interest rate—limited by law, and an equivalent loan to a large, distant corporation at much lower risk but equal return—doubtless a higher return if the lower administrative costs of loaning to large, well-financed corporations are included in the calculation. It can be said in this case that society has determined that excessive interest charges are more harmful than limited local support, and that consequently the loan should be given to the larger, distant firm.

Should we object to this decision? Suppose we believe that it is necessary, for the good of our society, that the formation of small, entrepreneurial companies be encouraged. It is often said that if we don't like a given action by a corporation, we should attempt to pass a law either prohibiting that action or encouraging an alternative action, and if we cannot get that law approved through our democratic processes, then we should accept the situation as it exists. That is, we should rely upon the law in our decisions, and agree that if a given act is legal it is "right" and if it is illegal it is "wrong," with the understanding that these determinations of right and wrong can be changed to reflect the majority views of the population. In the example just given, of a bank refusing to advance funds to a high-risk company in the local community and instead providing capital to a lower-risk corporation in a distant city, it would be fairly easy to design corrective legislation. Each bank within the state, or within the nation, could be required to invest a certain percentage of its funds within the communities from which it drew those funds from depositors. This is an aside, of course, but that was essentially the result of the prior laws in most states that prohibited branch banking; local banks were forced to invest within their communities because they had few customer contacts outside of those communities. Deregulation of banks, which ended such territorial restrictions, has also stopped the local service orientation of many financial institutions.

It would also be fairly easy to design a law that would encourage investments in higher-risk, smaller companies. It would be possible, for example, to reduce the risk by providing a governmental guarantee for a given percentage of the loan. This, in effect, was the result of the loan guarantee program of the Small Business Administration—a division of the federal government in the Department of Commerce. Through this program, the government would repurchase 90 percent of the unpaid balance of approved loans in the event of borrower default. Another approach would be to provide a subsidy to the bank or other financial institution to supplement the limited interest rates that may be charged to high-risk companies. That was the effect of the Area Development and Business Investment programs, also from the Small Business Administration, that provided funds at below-market rates to financial institutions for reinvestment in smaller, local firms.

AN EXAMPLE OF MORAL CHOICE

Now, let us return to the banker in the example that was used in the introduction to this chapter. He or she is faced with the decision whether or not to invest in a high-risk local company that will provide employment opportunities and other benefits within the community. Let us agree that this is an ethical dilemma, though in a somewhat mild form, for the choice is between the economic performance of the bank, as measured by potential profits, and the social performance of the same bank, stated in terms of obligations to members of the community. I have suggested that this is a somewhat "mild" ethical dilemma, for no one is going to be hurt very badly by the banker's decision. There will be some employment opportunities lost, and some tax payments not made, but no one will suffer physical harm, as in the unsafe discharge of toxic wastes, or endure emotional stress, as from unfair firing brought about by age, sex, or race discrimination. So, let us strengthen the dilemma. Let us assume that the local community is in an area of high unemployment, that new jobs are badly needed, and that the proposed company is in a labor-intensive, high-growth industry and might eventually create many new jobs. Let us assume that the alternative investment, the large corporation in a distant city, is in a capital-intensive industry and that it would create few new jobs. Let us go even further and assume that the product of the proposed local company is a needed health-care item that would reduce the pain and suffering of elderly patients in hospitals throughout the country, while the product of the alternative investment possibility is a line of high-calorie packaged "junk" foods with low nutritional value. Last, let us not assume but accept the fact that the funds available through the Small Business Administration have been sharply curtailed in recent years and that no governmental guarantee or interest subsidy is available to support the loan to the smaller company. Now we have the classic ethical dilemma: the choice between economic performance and social performance, complicated by extended consequences, uncertain outcomes, and career implications.

How would you decide if faced with this choice? If the banker replies to the founders of the new small company that he or she would very much like to help but that the law prevents an adequate return to compensate for the risk, that no federal guarantees or interest subsidies are available, and that bank officers are required by the legal system to minimize risks for their depositors, can the banker truly be said to be wrong? Of course, the usual response of most bankers to socially desirable but financially shaky loans is not to explain the reasoning that led to the loan rejection. Instead, they merely suggest that the potential borrowers should seek funds elsewhere—where they doubtless will receive exactly the same response.

The question of this chapter is not whether banks should make socially desirable but economically unfeasible loans. Obviously, if the loan cannot be repaid, no bank can make a series of those loans and remain in business. But that is not the issue here. The question is how to make the decision—what factors to consider and what standards to use—in attempting to arrive at a balance between economic performance and social performance. There does have to be a balance. A bank can't make a series of economically feasible but socially undesirable loans either and expect to have the society continue to exist in a form that will enable the bank to prosper. There has to be a limit on both sides. There has to be a balance, and the question is how to achieve that balance.

LAW AS COMBINED MORAL JUDGMENTS

In the last chapter, we looked at the argument that you could achieve the balance between economic and social performance by considering only financial factors and using only economic standards. According to this argument market forces lead inevitably towards maximum social benefits at minimum social costs (Pareto Optimality), and those benefits can then be distributed equitably by a political process. We found that argument wanting. In this chapter we will look at the argument that you should consider both financial and social factors but use legal standards—the requirements of the law—in making ethical or "balanced" choices.

Numerous attorneys and business executives believe that you can base ethical decisions and actions on the requirements of the law. These people would say that if a law is wrong, it should be changed, but that until it is changed it provides a meaningful guide for action. It provides this guide for action, they would add, because each law within a democratic society represents a combined moral judgment by members of our society on a given issue or problem. They will concede that you and I might not agree personally with that judgment on a particular issue, but they would claim that if managers follow the law on that issue, those managers cannot truly be said to be wrong in any ethical sense, since they are following the moral standards of a majority of their peers.

Advocates of the *rule of law*—a phrase that means the primacy of legal standards in any given social or economic choice—will normally admit that the combined moral judgments represented by the law form a minimal set of standards: the basic rules for living together within a society without infringing on the rights of others. "If you want to go beyond the basic rules of the law in your own decisions and actions," they might say, "we certainly have no objection." "But," they would add, "you cannot require us to go beyond the law, for then you are forcing us to adhere to your moral standards, not those of a majority of the population. We live in a democracy, so, if you don't like something that we are doing, gather together a majority of the voters and pass a law restricting those actions, and we will obey that law. Until then, however, our moral standards are fully as valid as your own, and ours have the support of the majority of the population, so please do not lecture us on your views of what is right or wrong, proper and improper, fair and unfair."

How do we respond to those statements? And if it is not possible to respond logically and convincingly, are we forced to accept the rule of law as determinant in most moral dilemmas? I think that it is necessary first to define the law, so that all of us will recognize that we are discussing the same set of concepts, and then to examine the process—or processes—involved in formulating the law. This examination will be generally the same as in Chapter 2, Managerial Ethics and Microeconomic Theory, in which we looked at the role of market forces as determinants for managerial decisions in ethical dilemmas. However, legal/social/political theory is much less complete than microeconomic theory and there are numerous alternative hypotheses that will have to be considered briefly. First, however, let us define the law and expand on what is meant by the *rule of law*.

DEFINITION OF THE LAW

The law can be defined as a consistent set of universal rules that are widely published, generally accepted, and usually enforced. These rules describe the ways in which people are required to act in their relationships with others within a society. They are requirements to act in a given way, not just expectations or suggestions or petitions to act in that way. There is an aura of insistency about the law; it defines what you *must* do.

These requirements to act, or more generally requirements *not* to act in a given way—most laws are negative commandments, telling us what we should *not* do in given situations—have a set of characteristics that were mentioned briefly above. The law was defined as a consistent, universal, published, accepted, and enforced set of rules. Let us look at each of these characteristics in greater detail.

Consistent

The requirements to act or not to act have to be consistent to be considered part of the law. That is, if two requirements contradict each other, both cannot be termed a law, because obviously people cannot obey both.

Universal

The requirements to act or not to act also have to be universal, or applicable to everyone with similar characteristics facing the same set of circumstances, to be considered part of the law. People tend not to obey rules that they believe are applied only to themselves and not to others.

Published

The requirements to act or not to act have to be published, in written form, so that they are accessible to everyone within the society, to be considered part of the law. Everyone may not have the time to read or be able to understand the rules, which tend to be complex due to the need to precisely define what constitute similar characteristics and the same set of circumstances. However, trained professionals—attorneys—are available to interpret and explain the law, so that ignorance of the published rules is not considered to be a valid excuse.

Accepted

The requirements to act or not to act in a given way have to be generally obeyed. If most members of the society do not voluntarily obey the law, too great a burden will be placed on the last provision, that of enforcement.

Enforced

The requirements to act or not to act in a given way have to be enforced. Members of society have to understand that they will be compelled to obey the law if they do not choose to do so voluntarily. People have to recognize that if they disobey the law, and if that disobedience is noted and can be proven, they will suffer some loss of convenience, time, money, freedom, or life. There is an aura of insistency about the law; there is also, or should be, an aura of inevitability; it defines what will happen if you don't follow the rules.

This set of rules that are consistent, universal, published, accepted, and enforced—which we call *law*—is supported by a framework of highly specialized social institutions. There are legislatures and councils to form the law; attorneys and paralegal personnel to explain the law; courts and agencies to interpret the law; sheriffs and police to enforce the law. These social institutions often change people's perception of the law because the institutions are obviously not perfect. The adversary relationships of the trial court often seem to ignore the provisions of consistency and universality and to focus on winning rather than justice. The enforcement actions of the police also often seem to be arbitrary and to concentrate on keeping the peace rather than maintaining equity. Let us admit that enforcing the law is a difficult and occasionally dangerous task. Let us also admit that interpreting the law, in court cases, often involves the award of large amounts of money, and that the potential gain or loss of these funds—with attorneys on each side being paid a substantial percentage of that loss or gain—has distorted the concept of the law as a set of published and accepted regulations. But we are looking at the law as an ideal concept of consistent and universal rules to guide managerial decisions, not as a flawed reality.

RELATIONSHIPS BETWEEN THE LAW AND MORAL STANDARDS

If the law is viewed in ideal terms as a set of universal and consistent rules to govern human conduct within society, the question is whether we can accept these rules—flawed though they may be by pragmatic problems in interpretation and enforcement—as representing the collective moral judgment of members of our society. If we can, then we have the standards to guide managerial decisions and actions—even though these standards may be at a minimal level. If we cannot accept the set of rules as representing the collective moral judgment of our society, then we will have to look elsewhere for our standards. In considering the possible relationship between moral judgments and legal requirements, there would seem to be three conclusions that can be reached fairly quickly:

1. The requirements of the law overlap to a considerable extent but do not duplicate the probable moral standards of society. Clearly, a person who violates the federal law against bank robbery also violates the moral standard against theft. And it is easy to show that the laws governing sexual conduct, narcotics usage, product liability, and contract adherence are similar to the moral beliefs that probably are held by a majority of people in our society. I think that we can agree that in a democratic society, the legal requirements do reflect many of the basic values of the citizens, and that there is an area of overlap between the law and morality (see Figure 3–1).

But the area of overlap is not complete. There are some laws that are morally inert, with no ethical content whatever. The requirement that we drive on the right-hand side of the road, for example, is neither inherently right nor inherently wrong; it is just essential that we all agree on which side we are going to drive. There are also some laws that are morally repugnant. Until the early 1960s, some areas of the United States legally required racial discrimination (segregated education, housing, and travel accommodations), and slavery was legally condoned just 100 years earlier. Finally, there are some moral standards that have no legal standing whatever. We all object to lying, but truthfulness is not required by law except in a court, under oath, and in a few other specific instances such as employment contracts and property sales.

People who believe in the rule of law and accept legal regulations as the best means of governing human conduct within society would respond by saying that it is not at all clear that racial segregation was deplored by a majority of the population prior to 1962, or even that slavery was considered unconscionable before

FIGURE 3–1
Overlap between Moral Standards and Legal Requirements

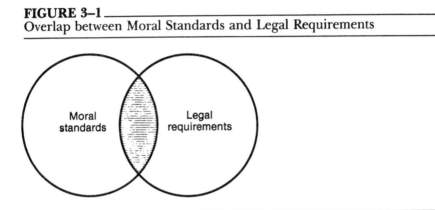

1862. In a much lighter vein, concerning lying, they might even claim that most people have become accustomed to, and perhaps are amused by, a reasonable lack of truthfulness in advertising messages and political discourse. Moral standards, they would say, are difficult to determine, and we must be careful not to infer that our standards represent those held by a majority of the population.

2. The requirements of the law tend to be negative, while the standards of morality more often are positive. In the law, we are forbidden to assault, rob, or defame each other, but we are not required to help people, even in extreme situations. There is no law, for example, that we must go to the aid of a drowning child. Here, we do have a situation where the moral standards of the majority can be inferred, for doubtless 99.9 percent of the adult population within the United States would go to the aid of a drowning child, to the limit of their ability. People who support the rule of law, however, would say that this instance does not indicate a lack of relationship between moral standards and legal requirements; it only indicates the difficulty of translating one into the other when a positive—compassionate or charitable—act is needed. How, they would question, can you define in consistent and universal terms what is meant by assistance, the characteristics of the person who is to provide that assistance, and the circumstances under which it will be required? This, they would conclude, is just another illustration that the law represents the minimum set of standards to govern behavior in society and that actions beyond that minimum have to come from individual initiative, not legal force.

3. The requirements of the law tend to lag behind the apparent moral standards of society. Slavery, of course, is the most odious example, but sexual and racial discrimination, environmental pollution, and foreign bribery can all be cited as moral problems that were belatedly remedied by legislation. Advocates of the rule of law would say, however, that the evidence of a delay between apparent moral consensus and enacted legal sanctions does not necessarily indicate a lack of relationship between legal requirements and moral standards. It only serves to confirm that relationship, they would claim, for laws controlling discrimination, pollution, and bribery were eventually passed.

None of these arguments—that legal requirements overlap but do not duplicate moral standards, or that the legal requirements appear in different forms (negative rather than positive) and at different times (sequential rather than concurrent). None really helps to determine whether the law really does represent collective moral judgments by members of a democratic society and consequently can serve to guide managerial decisions and actions. We can easily say that the law does not represent our moral judgment in a given situation, but how can we say that the law in that instance does not represent the moral judgment of a majority of our peers? For that, I think, we have to follow through the process by which our society has developed the law as a universal and consistent set of rules to govern human conduct.

FORMATION OF THE LAW: INDIVIDUAL PROCESSES

Law is obviously a dynamic entity, for the rules change over time. Think of the changes that have occurred in the laws governing employment, for example, or pollution. This is essentially the same point that was made previously, that there seems to be a time lag between changes in moral standards and changes in legal requirements, but actions that were considered to be legal twenty years ago—such as racial and sexual discrimination in hiring, or the discharge of chemical wastes into lakes and streams, are now clearly illegal. The question is whether these changes in the law came from changes in the moral standards of a majority of our population through a social and political process, and consequently whether the law does represent the collective moral standards of our society. The social and political process by which the changing moral standards of individual human beings are alleged to become institutionalized into the formal legal framework of society is lengthy and complex, but a simplified version can be shown in graphic form (see Figure 3–2).

Each individual within society has a set of norms, beliefs, and values that together form his or her moral standards. Norms, of course, are criteria of behavior. They are the ways an individual expects all people to act, when faced with a given situation. Foreign students from certain Asiatic countries, for example, bow slightly when addressing a university professor; the bow is their norm or expectation of behavior given that situation. University faculty members within the United States are generally somewhat annoyed when this occurs; their norm or expectation of behavior in that situation is considerably less formal and more egalitarian. The depth of the bow and the degree of annoyance both decline over time as the expectations of behavior on both sides are modified through learning.

Another example of a norm of behavior is considerably less facetious and more relevant to the discussion of moral standards and the law. Most people expect that others, when they meet them, should not cause them injury. Norms are expectations of the ways people ideally should act, not anticipations of the ways people really will act. A person who holds a norm against assault and robbery—as most of us do—will not ordinarily walk down a dark street in the warehouse district of a city at three in the morning; he or she feels that people *should* not assault and rob each other, not that they *will* not do so.

Norms are expectations of proper behavior, not requirements for that behavior. This is the major difference between a norm and a law; the norm is not published, may not be obeyed, and cannot be enforced—except by the sanctions of a small group whose members hold similar norms and use such penalties as disapproval or exclusion. Norms also are often neither consistent nor universal. The person who actually commits a crime in the warehouse district at three in the morning, feeling it permissible to assault and rob someone else given the situation and need, doubtless would feel outraged if assaulted and robbed in the same place and at the same time the next night. Norms are just the way we feel about behavior; often they are neither logically consistent nor universally applied because we have never thought through the reasons we hold them.

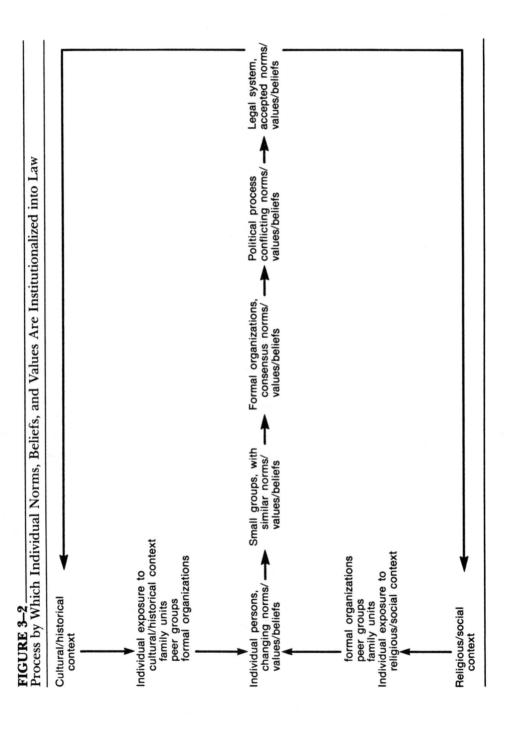

FIGURE 3-2
Process by Which Individual Norms, Beliefs, and Values Are Institutionalized into Law

Beliefs are criteria of thought; they are the ways an individual expects people to think about given concepts. I believe in participatory democracy, for example, and I expect others to recognize the worth of that concept and accept it as a form of government. I believe in environmental preservation also, and I expect other people to recognize the importance of that idea and accept it as a goal worth working towards.

Beliefs are different from norms in that they involve no action—no overt behavior towards others—just an abstract way of thinking that tends to support an individual's norms. Asiatic students who bow to American professors believe, it is alleged, in a hierarchical society, with definite gradations between older faculty and younger students. People who hold the norm that others should not assault and rob them, even on darkened streets and in deserted neighborhoods, generally believe in the worth of human beings and the preservation of personal property. In one last example, the norm that a company should not bury toxic wastes in leaking 55-gallon drums is associated with beliefs about the benefits of a clean environment and the adverse effects of chemical pollution upon individual health.

Values, the last third of this pattern of personal criteria that together form the moral standards of an individual, are the rankings or priorities that a person establishes for his or her norms and beliefs. Most people do not consider that all their norms and beliefs are equal in importance; generally there are some that seem much more important than others. The important norms and beliefs are the ones that a person "values," or holds in high esteem.

Values often are controversial. Why? Because a norm or belief that one person holds in high esteem can conflict with a different norm or belief that another person holds in equally high esteem. Generally there will be little accommodation or compromise, because each person attaches great importance to his or her criteria of behavior—ways in which people ought to act—and of belief—ways in which people ought to think. We live in a pluralistic society, with numerous cultural traditions, and in a secular nation, with no accepted or endorsed religious heritage; consequently we have to live with the fact that norms, beliefs, and values will differ among individuals. These differences can and do lead to conflicts.

The norms, beliefs, and values of an individual together form that person's moral standards. Moral standards are our means of judging whether an act that affects others is "right" or "wrong," and they are based upon our personal valuation or ranking of norms—criteria of behavior—and beliefs—criteria of thought. For example, I value highly my norm of nonaggressive behavior between members of our society; if I come out of my house on a summer morning and you hit me on the head and steal my wallet, I am going to consider what you have done to be "wrong." I value less highly my belief in the benefits of a clean environment; if I come out of my house the next day and find you pouring used motor oil down the drain in the street, I am going to think of you as a fairly despicable person, for I would consider that act to be "wrong" also, but less wrong than your previous assault and robbery.

Moral standards—the criteria we use for judging whether an act that impacts others is right or wrong—for now can be considered to be subjective, that is, the result of each individual's emotional preferences among a range of possible norms and beliefs. In the next chapter, Managerial Ethics and Normative Philosophy, we will consider the possibility that moral standards might be seen as objective, or rationally derived from a single fundamental norm or absolute belief. An example of a fundamental norm would be, Always act to generate the greatest good for the greatest number; an example of an absolute belief would be, Justice is the basic essential for a cooperative society. A fundamental norm or absolute belief, if accepted by an individual, would objectively determine that person's complete set of moral standards, because all of his or her other norms and beliefs could be logically derived, in an orderly ranking or value system, from that single principle or truth. A fundamental norm or absolute belief, if accepted by all members of society, would lead to consistent moral standards throughout society, for the same reason. For the present discussion, however, it is necessary to admit that our society lacks such a single principle or truth. This is not to say that we should not have an accepted basis for consistent moral standards; it is just to say that we presently do not have that accepted basis.

FORMATION OF THE LAW: GROUP PROCESSES

Each individual has a set of norms, beliefs, and values that subjectively determine his or her moral standards. These moral standards are at least partially unique to each person, as they are based upon emotional selection rather than rational determination. Most adult members of society recognize their individual set of standards, but few of us have examined or considered these standards beyond a general understanding of mutual reciprocity and social continuance. "I should not assault and rob others because then they would feel free to assault and rob me" and "I should not assault and rob others because no society can continue to exist if assault and robbery are constant occurrences" are both moral statements, though based upon slightly different sets of norms, beliefs, and values. "I should not assault and rob others because I might get caught and put in jail" is more a legal concern than a moral standard, and it is based upon a very different set of norms, beliefs, and values.

Each individual develops his or her set of norms, beliefs, and values through exposure to the cultural/religious context, the social/political context, and the economic/technological context. *Context* means the general background or surrounding environment of a situation; the literal derivation of the word is from the Latin "woven together," and that almost exactly conveys the meaning that is intended here. Each society has a background or environment that consists of interwoven threads from religious teachings, cultural traditions, economic conditions, technological developments, social organizations, and political processes. The interwoven nature of the context within which individual choices on norms, beliefs, and values are made ensures that all of these factors interact. Technological changes in communication bring political changes in governance, which cause economic changes in spending and taxation patterns, which eventually result in cultural changes in personal life-style. The exact relationships between economic, technological, social, political, cultural, and religious factors are not known, nor can their combined influences upon an individual's norms, beliefs, and values be predicted with accuracy. But the relationships and influences can easily be observed. Think of the changing status of women, for example, which must have had some origin in the economic shift from heavy manufacturing and mining to knowledge-based and service industries, in the technological development of better birth-control methods, and in the social expansion of educational opportunities. Another illustration of a change in norms, beliefs, and values would be the widespread concern with preservation of the physical environment that developed during the 1960s, and was doubtless influenced by the economic prosperity and political activism of that period.

FORMATION OF THE LAW: SOCIAL PROCESSES

All individuals within a society do not have the same exposures to economic, technological, social, political, cultural, and religious factors. Such exposures come from individual positions, family units, peer groups, and formal organizations. For example, a steel worker who has been unemployed for a number of years due to the closing of a steel mill is directly exposed to the economic reality of international competition; children of the steel worker are indirectly but forcefully exposed through the family unit; associates of the steel worker are indirectly and more lightly exposed through peer groups such as neighborhood associations or social clubs and through formal organizations such as churches and banks. The norms, beliefs, and values of people throughout the industrialized cities that were heavily dependent upon steel, such as Buffalo, Pittsburgh, and Youngstown, have changed over the past 10 years, but to varying degrees, depending upon each individual's exposure to the underlying economic and technological factors.

The changing norms, beliefs, and values of individuals within society do, in a democratic society, have an apparent though delayed impact upon the law. This impact would appear to be the result of both social and political processes. The social process involves, basically, an accretion of power. People with similar norms, beliefs, and values tend to become associated in small groups; it is just natural to join others who have parallel views. These small groups generally are part of much larger organizations, such as business firms, labor unions, political parties, charitable agencies, religious institutions, and veteran's associations, and these larger organizations over time either achieve an acceptable compromise on norms, beliefs, and values, or split into smaller organizations that can achieve such a compromise. There are alternative theories on the means by which this compromise is formed: autocratic decision, bureaucratic adjustment, coalition bargaining, or collective choice. Doubtless all these methods are employed to different degrees in different organi-

zations, but the outcome that can be observed is that many organizations do display a culture of shared norms, beliefs, and
values that gradually changes over time.

FORMATION OF THE LAW: POLITICAL PROCESSES

The political process by which the norms, beliefs, and values
held by organizations, groups, and individuals are institutionalized into law can be seen basically as a means of resolving conflict. Organizations, groups, and individuals obviously have
different opinions on what should be done now (norms) and
what should be accomplished in the future (beliefs), and these
different views have to be reconciled into consistent and universal rules to be effective. Again, there are alternative theories on
the ways by which this is done: presidential leadership, institutional compromise, congressional bargaining, and constituent
pressure. The terms would differ at the federal, state, and local
levels, but the process doubtless remains approximately the
same. The leader, whether president, governor, or mayor, can
speak of long-term objectives and attempt to gather support, but
he or she has little direct influence on the law-making mechanism. Governmental departments and agencies and nongovern-
mental lobbying organizations provide the support with
information, arguments, and campaign assistance but often must
compromise their positions to work jointly and not cancel out
each other's influence. Elected representatives are formally assigned responsibility for the formulation of laws in a representative system, but issues differ by section of the country, segment
of the population and sector of the economy, and consequently
there often seems to be bargaining to establish coalitions to pass
most legislation. The public, of course, can express opinions on
potential laws by voting for some administrators and all legislators, and indirectly through public surveys, letters, and the
media.

The political process by which laws are enacted represents a
complex series of interactions. Doubtless no one except a member of Congress or one of the state legislatures fully appreciates
the extent and time demands of the formal hearings, office
meetings, and committee reports, the constant interruptions and
informal exchanges that occur in hallways, parking lots, and eve-
ning receptions, and the honest efforts that are made to sum-

marize opinions from the electorate expressed in letters, telephone calls, and the media. All of these help to form the opinions of the legislators. It is easy to be cynical when thinking of the political process, particularly when the high cost of election campaigns is considered and the need to raise money to finance those campaigns is included, but it is difficult to invent a better process than representative democracy.

CONCLUSIONS ON THE RULE OF LAW AS THE BASIS FOR MORAL CHOICE

The question now is whether these social and political processes, lengthy and complex though they may be, truly do serve to combine the personal moral standards of a majority of our population, slowly and gradually, into universal legal requirements. That is, does the law actually represent the collective moral judgment of a majority of our population, or does it just consist of a set of official commands determined by unresponsive legislators? The view that the law does represent collective moral judgment is certainly appealing. However, there would seem to be problems in the transfer from individual moral standards to universal legal requirements at each of the stages in the social and political process.

1. The moral standards of members of society may be based upon a lack of information relative to issues of corporate conduct. Most people were apparently unaware of the payments of large foreign bribes until the revelations of the Lockheed case and the subsequent Securities and Exchange Commission study. Many people now may be unaware of the magnitude of the toxic waste-disposal problem, with 231 million metric tons being produced annually. It is difficult for personal moral standards to influence the law if relevant information is missing.

2. The moral standards of members of society may be diluted in the formation of small groups. People with similar norms, beliefs, and values tend to become associated in small groups, but these standards generally are not precisely similar among all members, and compromises have to be made. Further, many small groups act from motives other than morality; economic benefits and professional prestige often seem to be stressed. It is difficult for personal moral standards to influence the law if they are not conveyed accurately.

3. The moral standards of members of society may be misrepresented in the consensus of large organizations. Many organizations do share norms, beliefs, and values, but there is no evidence that each individual and each group within the organization has equal influence, or even equal weighted influence, in determining that consensus. This can be seen in the norms, beliefs, and values of many nonprofit organizations such as hospitals and universities; the standards of the professional personnel—the physicians and the faculty—often seem to predominate.

4. The moral standards of members of society may be misrepresented in the formulation of the laws. This is the same point that was made above in shaping the consensus of an organization, though on a larger scale. There is no guarantee that all organizations have equal influence, or even equal influence weighted by size, in determining the law. This can be seen in the provisions of much tax legislation; certain organizations always seem to be favored.

5. The legal requirements formed through the political process are often incomplete or imprecise and have to be supplemented by judicial court decisions or administrative agency actions. This can be seen in both product liability cases and equal employment reviews; the meaning and the application of the law have to be clarified outside of the legislative process. It is difficult for personal moral standards to influence the law if they are considered only indirectly—if at all—in two of the means of formulating that law.

What can we say in summary? We can observe that there obviously is an overlap between the moral standards and the legal requirements of our society—the federal law against bank robbery and the moral standard against stealing, for example. And we can see that some changes in the norms, beliefs, and values of individual members of society are eventually reflected by changes in the law—the Foreign Corrupt Practices Act and the Federal Air Pollution Control Act, for example. But we will have to admit that there is no direct relationship in all instances. The social and political processes by which the law is formulated are too complex and too cumbersome—and perhaps too subject to manipulation—for changes in people's norms, beliefs, and values to be directly translated into changes in that set of universal and consistent rules that we call law. Consequently, we cannot view this set of rules as representing the complete collective moral judgment of our society, and therefore we cannot rely totally on the rules when confronted by an ethical dilemma.

The law is a guide to managerial decisions and actions, but it is not enough. And certainly, the absence of a law is not enough to excuse some of those decisions and actions. We need something more. In the next chapter we will look at the fundamental norms and absolute values of normative philosophy as a possible means of providing that "something more."

CASES

Pollution in Louisiana

The first oil well was drilled in Louisiana in 1901. Two brothers from Ohio, veterans of the Spindletop oil field of Texas, paid a farmer $10 for drilling rights after promising to rid his rice fields of the black ooze that damaged his crops. They hit the first gusher. Large oil companies quickly followed the individual wildcatters, and Louisiana became one of the major petroleum-producing regions of the country. In the following 84 years, to 1985, it is estimated that 12 billion barrels of oil and 113 billion cubic feet of natural gas have been produced. This production has brought personal wealth, industrial development, and extensive pollution.

It isn't unusual to find contaminated water here in the state's industrial, oil-refining, and petrochemical corridor (along the Mississippi River, near Baton Rouge). Tons of waste containing potentially toxic heavy metals and organic chemicals are generated daily, and have been for decades.

But Louisiana's water problems aren't confined to the industrial zones. In one town in the coastal marshes of South Louisiana, a test of 84 water wells found that 81 contained heavy metals. The water in another community is so briny that drinking fountains are stained white. In some swamps, groves of cypress stand dead.

These are areas of heavy oil and gas production, where thousands of open waste pits brim with brine from far underground and with the soup of chemicals poured into wells during drilling. Other waste sludge is sunk in old wells for disposal, spread over adjoining land or, if the drilling site is off-shore, simply dumped into the water.[1]

There are two major sources of the pollution associated with oil and gas production. The first is salt. Most petroleum reserves are found in salt domes, and it is necessary to drill through the salt to reach the oil or gas. Tons of brine are brought to the surface for every well that is completed, and additional tons of brine, as much as eight times the amount of oil and gas, are brought to the surface during production. The brine is normally pumped into "disposal" wells that have been drilled nearby into a porous rock formation.

The second major source of pollution is the drilling "mud" that is used to lubricate the drilling bit, flush the drill cuttings to the surface, and line the sides of the well. The mud is compounded differently for the drilling conditions at each site, but it consists generally of a mixture of viscous clays, weighting agents, and chemicals. The weighting agents—such heavy metals as barium, chromium, arsenic, lead, titanium, and zinc—are added to help solidify rock formations and keep the walls of the well from collapsing. The chemicals used include carbolic acid, caustic soda, ammonia bisulfite, zinc chromate, formaldehyde, asbestos, asphalt, and phenols. Approximately 1 million pounds of mud are used to drill a typical well of 10,000-foot depth.

One third of the drilling mud remains underground, forced into the rock formations; the rest comes to the surface and is recycled until it becomes so laden with the drill waste that it must be replaced. If the well is a dry hole, the used drilling mud is commonly pumped into it. For producing wells, the used mud is generally abandoned in an earthen pit about one acre in size. This same pit is used to hold the waste oil and other contaminants generated during the production life of the well. There are an estimated 13,000 oil field pits in Louisiana.

Leakage of salt from the disposal wells and leaching of the heavy metals and chemicals from the waste pits are gradually polluting the underground water supplies. Tests have shown unacceptable levels of salt, heavy metals, and chemicals—two to three times the allowable federal standard—in the drinking water of rural farms and small towns throughout South

Louisiana. These contaminants have had an apparent, though unproven, impact upon health.

> . . . . unusual levels of illness are showing up in much of South Louisiana. No one can demonstrate whether any of the illness is linked to oil and gas activity or to the area's extensive water pollution. But concern is mounting, and some of the cases are striking.
>
> The area around Kaplan, Louisiana, where Jerome Vincent lives, is a site of many old and new oil and gas wells. Superior Oil Company sank another one, a very deep dry hole, in the rice field behind his home four years ago. It left behind some leaky barrels and three open waste pits.
>
> In May, 1983, a private laboratory tested Mr. Vincent's well water and found it contained chromium, a metal that is sometimes dumped in oil wells during drilling and that toxicology manuals link with cancer. His well's chromium level was slightly higher than the federal limit for public drinking water systems.
>
> Tests by the state health department found chromium-rich sludge in Mr. Vincent's water-well pipe. The private lab tested sludge from one of the waste pits, and found its chromium level to be more than 2,700 times the concentration in Mr. Vincent's water.
>
> In June, 1983, Mr. Vincent's 40-year-old wife died of leukemia. Two months later, his 62-year-old father, who lived next door, died of pancreatic cancer. Then this year his 21-year-old son died of cardiopulmonary arrest associated with fatty infiltration (cancer) of the liver.

*　*　*　*　*

> In adjoining Cameron Parish (county) Annette Baccigalopi worries about an oil waste disposal well a few hundred yards from her home, a well the state temporarily closed this year because of possible leaks. Her anxiety seems understandable; in the past several years, cancer has taken the lives of her father, her father-in-law, her brother-in-law, and her daughter's father-in-law, all from the same area. Her mother-in-law has cancer now, and her mother and a cousin have had cancer operations.[2]

The ten counties in South Louisiana, the center for oil and gas production in the state, now rank in the top 5 percent nationwide for deaths caused by cancer.

Exercise. What should have been done to prevent this contamination of the drinking water supplies of South Louisiana? Why, in your opinion, was nothing done?

Footnotes

1. *The Wall Street Journal,* Oct. 23, 1984, p. 1.
2. Ibid.

Truthfulness in Advertising

Advertising claims may be totally inaccurate ("sticker price is a low $5,998" may omit all transportation costs, state taxes, dealer charges, and factory options, which together add 25 percent to 30 percent to the price of a car). Other claims are greatly exaggerated ("12-hour relief from sore throat pain"), verbally misleading ("you'll have to eat 12 bowls of Shredded Wheat to get the vitamins and nutrition in one bowl of Total"), or visually misleading (healthy, active people shown in pleasant social situations to advertise liquor, beer, or cigarettes).

Exercise. From magazines, newspapers, or television, select an advertisement you believe to be untruthful. Be prepared to describe why you feel the claims are untruthful and into what group (inaccurate, exaggerated, or misleading) you think they fall.

General Motors and "Poletown"

General Motors in 1980 was reeling under the combined impact of a national recession and international competition; the company lost $1,147 million in that year, before receipt of a refund for prior year's taxes. Senior executives realized that they would have to redesign their car lines, to emphasize smaller, lighter, more fuel-efficient models, and should also reconstruct their manufacturing plants to reduce costs and improve quality. They allocated $4.5 billion to renovate or replace nine of the oldest facilities.

In Detroit, it was determined that the 60-year-old Cadillac assembly factory, would have to be completely rebuilt. The problem was that there was not enough land on the site. The new assembly facility was to be modeled on a large and extremely efficient plant, located in Oklahoma City, that had 3 million square feet on one floor to simplify handling, and that required between 450 and 500 acres for the building plus the associated car loading, parts storage, rail yard, employee parking, and highway-access areas. The company notified the city of Detroit that it would be forced to move unless a suitable site could be found.

Detroit at this time was also suffering from the effects of the national recession and the problems of the domestic car manufacturers. Unemployment in the city was over 18 percent—nearly 30 percent among blacks—and the 6,000 jobs and substantial tax payments represented by the new assembly plant were very attractive. City officials helped in the search for a suitable site; it had to be large, a minimum of 450 acres, with good access to rail lines and highways.

Detroit is an aging city, with many abandoned factories and rundown neighborhoods, but apparently no site was large enough, or close enough to the transportation networks, to justify the investment. Finally, however, the director of the Commission on Economic Development, Emmet Moten, was able to suggest a 465.5 acre site known as "Dodge Main" because of an abandoned Chrysler Corporation factory on a portion of the land. The site had good rail and highway connections, and it was close enough to the existing Cadillac assembly plant so that the workers would be able to transfer without inconvenience. The obsolete factory could be cleared with a Housing and Urban Development grant from the federal government, and Conrail was willing to rebuild the rail facilities. In short, the site was ideal except for one problem; it required taking, by right of eminent domain, a portion of an ethnic community known as "Poletown."

Poletown was a residential and commercial area that had been settled in the 1920s by emigrants from Poland and Germany. Sixty years later, some of the homes and businesses had deteriorated, but others were still well maintained. There was a Poletown Neighborhood Council that had borrowed money, and received grants and donations, for revitalization of the business district, and there were clubs, churches, and other social groups

that were active within the community. While the Polish population and character remained strong, the area was integrated,
with an estimated 40 percent of the families being black; race
relationships were felt to be good, and Poletown was known,
within the city of Detroit, as an integrated area that worked.

The construction of the new Cadillac assembly plant would
involve moving 3,348 people from Poletown and razing 1,176
buildings, including 669 single-family homes, 343 two-family
homes, 114 local businesses, and 50 schools, churches, and community buildings. Many of the residents wanted to cooperate
with the city and were willing to move, pending satisfactory set-
tlements on the value of their homes and businesses, but a minority, less than 1,000 people, declared their opposition to the
project and said that they would fight through the courts for the
right to remain in their own homes. Some of the older residents,
of course, had built those homes and had extensive family mem-
ories associated with the structures. Attempts to redesign the assembly plant to require less land usage ran into immediate
technical problems, and efforts to expand in other directions involved the displacement of even larger numbers of people.

Both Thomas Murphy, chairman of the General Motors Corporation, and Emmet Moten, director of the Detroit Committee
on Economic Development, were troubled by the decision to
force people to leave their homes:

> Now, General Motors didn't select the site. We did make the de-
> cision to relocate and stay in the Detroit area—and we did ask the
> city to help find a site of the size we required to build a modern
> assembly facility. Perhaps the easy way—if we weren't concerned
> about the community and the people—would have been to move to
> a location outside of this area—out of the state if necessary. But I
> want to tell you today there is only one reason for our decision,
> and that is this: We want to do what is right for every community
> where we operate. So we have chosen to stay—if there is any way
> we can—because we feel we have a commitment to this community,
> to our employees, and to all the people in this area.[1]

* * * * *

> We're fighting for our damned lives. It used to be that the pri-
> vate sector could do everything for themselves. But that's changed
> in the last four or five years and more cities are helping industry
> now by assembling land and providing "gap" financing. Other cities

have had smaller problems, but in Detroit, we've been hurt with a major economic problem as a result of the downturn in the auto industry.[2]

Condemnation proceedings were started, and legal opposition did develop as expected. In 1981, the Michigan Supreme Court ruled that the City of Detroit could use the public right of eminent domain to take property for private use because of the need for new industrial development to revitalize local industries. People were removed from their homes and businesses. In a particularly poignant and distressing finale, elderly parishioners were forcefully removed from their church, so that it might be destroyed for the new Cadillac assembly plant.

Exercise. Assume that you were a member of the Board of Directors of General Motors in 1980. What factors would you have considered in reaching a decision on the "Poletown" plant? List those factors in your order of importance. What does that list say about your norms, beliefs, and values?

Footnotes

1. Statement by Thomas A. Murphy, Chairman, General Motors Corp., before the Rotary Club of Hamtramck, Hamtramck, Mich., October 30, 1980, p. 5.

2. Emmet Moten, Director, Detroit Council on Economic Development, *Detroit News*, September 2, 1980, p. 3A.

CHAPTER 4

Managerial Ethics and Normative Philosophy

The ethical dilemma in management centers on the continual conflict, or on the continual potential for that conflict, that exists between the economic and the social performance of an organization. Business firms have to operate profitably or they will not survive over the long term; that is their economic performance. Business firms also have to recognize their obligations to employees, customers, suppliers, distributors, stockholders, and the general public; that is their social performance. The problem—and the essence of the ethical dilemma in management—is that sometimes improvements in economic performance—increases in sales or decreases in costs—can be made only at the expense of one or more of the groups to whom the organization has some form of obligation. The economies of scale that follow a merger can be achieved only if the surplus employees are discharged or demoted. The benefits of direct factory-to-store distribution can be realized only if the existing wholesalers are replaced. The advantages of hydroelectric power can be realized only if a river valley is flooded and local residents are forced to move.

How do we decide when faced with these issues? How do we find the balance between economic performance and social performance that is "right" and "proper" and "just"? There are only three forms of analysis—ways of thinking about the dilemma and arriving at the balance—that can be used:

- *Economic analysis,* based on impersonal market forces. The belief is that a manager should always act to maximize revenues and minimize costs, for this strategy, over the long term, will produce the greatest material benefits for society, and those benefits can be equitably distributed by political, not economic, means. As we saw, there are both practical and theoretical problems with that approach, so we cannot rely on economic analysis to resolve ethical conflicts; it certainly helps to know the financial revenues and costs, but something more is needed.
- *Legal analysis,* based on impersonal social and political processes. The belief is that a manager should always act to obey the law, for the law within a democracy represents the collective moral judgment of members of society. Again, there are both practical and theoretical problems with that view, so we cannot rely on legal analysis, either by itself or in conjunction with economic analysis, to resolve ethical conflicts. It certainly helps to know the legality of a situation, but something even further is needed.
- *Philosophic analysis,* based on rational thought processes. The view is that a manager should always act in accordance with either a single principle of behavior or a single statement of belief that is "right" and "proper" and "just" in and by itself. This is "moral reasoning"; logically working from a first principle through to a decision on the duties we owe to others. There are some problems here also, though perhaps not as serious as in the other two instances.

Moral reasoning requires an understanding of normative philosophy. It is not possible to summarize normative philosophy in a single chapter—just as, quite frankly, it is not really possible to summarize microeconomic relationships or social/political processes in a single chapter—but it is possible to convey some of the basic concepts and methods, provided the reader is interested and willing to think about them. I assume that you are interested or you would not have gotten this far.

DEFINITION OF NORMATIVE PHILOSOPHY

Philosophy is the study of thought and conduct; normative philosophy is the study of the proper thought and conduct; that is, how we should behave. Normative philosophers have been looking at these issues for more than 2,400 years—since the time of Plato, who lived from 427 to 347 B.C. They have attempted to establish a logical thought process, based upon an incontrovertible first principle, that would determine whether an act were "right" or "wrong," "good" or "evil," "fair" or "unfair." They have not been successful—otherwise all that would be needed would be to quote the sources and state the findings—but many of their concepts and methods are relevant to managerial ethics. All hard ethical decisions are compromises, between economic and social performance in the case of a business firm, between wants and duties in the case of an individual. Normative philosophy provides some help in making those compromises, but that help is not as extensive as one might wish. Here, then, is an introduction to the normative philosophy of morality and ethics.

First, there is a difference between morality and ethics. Morality refers to the standards of behavior by which people are judged, and particularly to the standards of behavior by which people are judged in their relationships with others. A person in the midst of a desert, isolated from anyone else, might act in a way that was immature, demeaning, or stupid, but he or she could not truly be said to have acted immorally since that behavior could have no impact upon others, unless it were to waste water or other resources needed by travelers in the future. Ethics, on the other hand, encompasses the system of beliefs that supports a particular view of morality. If I believe that a person should not smoke in a crowded room, it is because I have accepted the research findings of some scientists and the published statements of the Surgeon General that tobacco smoke is harmful; my acceptance of those findings is my ethic, for that particular situation. *Ethics* is normally used in the plural form since most people have a system of interrelated beliefs rather than a single opinion. The difference between morality and ethics is easy to remember if one speaks of moral standards of behavior and ethical systems of belief, and I will use those terms in this discussion.

ETHICAL RELATIVISM

The next issue to be addressed in this description of the techniques of moral reasoning is that of ethical relativism. The question here is very basic: Are there objective universal principles upon which one can construct an ethical system of belief that is applicable to all groups in all cultures at all times? Moral standards of behavior differ between groups within a single culture, between cultures, and between times. This is obvious. For example, within the contemporary United States, moral standards for decisions on product safety differ between the leaders of consumer interest groups and the executives of major industrial corporations, and it is probable that these standards of product safety would differ even more greatly between the United States and the Middle East, or between the contemporary period and the late nineteenth century. The ethical systems of belief supporting those moral standards of behavior also differ; each group, in each country, in each time period, can usually give a very clear explanation of the basis for its actions. To continue the earlier example, representatives of consumer interest groups can provide a perfectly logical reason for their support of a mandatory requirement that air bags be installed in passenger cars, and managerial personnel from the automotive manufacturing companies can offer an equally logical reason for their opposition to such a requirement. Both sides base their arguments on a system of beliefs as to what is best for the national society, but unfortunately those beliefs differ. I think we can all agree that among the most irritating aspects of the debate over ethical issues such as product safety are the attitudes of personal self-righteousness and the implications of opponent self-interest that seem to pervade all these discussions. Both sides assume that their systems of belief are so widely held, and so obviously logical, that their opponents have to be small-minded and illiberal; they do not recognize the legitimate differences that can exist between ethical systems as to what is "right" or "proper" or "good" for the country.

The question in ethical relativism is not whether different moral standards and ethical beliefs exist; they obviously do, and we all have experiences to confirm that fact. The question is whether there is any commonality that overrides the differences. In the mixed chorus of competing moral standards and diverse ethical systems, can we discern any single principle that unifies them all, or are we left with the weak and unsatisfactory conclusion that all ethical systems are equally valid, and that a person's choice has to be relative to his or her upbringing or education or position or country or culture. If all ethical systems are equally valid, then no firm moral judgments can be made about individual behavior, and we are all on our own, to do as we like to others, within economic and legal constraints.

Fortunately, there is one principle that does seem to exist across all groups, cultures, and times and that does form part of every ethical system; that is the belief that members of a group bear some form of responsibility for the well-being of other members of that group. There is a widespread recognition that men and women are social beings, that cooperation is necessary for survival, and that some standards of behavior are needed to ensure that cooperation. In one of the most famous statements in ethical philosophy, Thomas Hobbes (1588–1679) argued that if everyone acted on the basis of his or her own self-interest and ignored the well-being of others, life would be "solitary, nasty, brutish, and short."

People in all cultures, even the most primitive, do not act solely for their own self-interest, and people in those cultures understand that standards of behavior are needed to promote cooperation and ensure survival. These standards of behavior can be either negative—it is considered wrong to harm other members of the group—or positive—it is considered right to help other group members—but they do exist and can be traced in both sociological and anthropological studies. Consequently, the important question in moral relativism is not whether your moral standards are as good as mine; it is whether your moral standards that benefit society are as good as mine that benefit society.[1] The second question is very different from the first; it forces both of us to justify our standards relative to a principle that does extend over groups, cultures, and times. We can say that our definitions of what is "right" differ, and we can each act in accordance with those definitions and believe that we are morally correct; yet the way in which we determine what is "right" is the same.

The fact that there can be two different moral standards, both of which can be considered to be "right," is confusing to many people. Let me try to clarify this apparent paradox with an example, and we will use the familiar example of the Brazilian customs. Let us say that I am from that South American country, and I believe it is morally acceptable to pay small bribes to the customs agents in order to expedite import clearance and shipment. You, on the other hand, are from the United States, and you find the practice to be morally unacceptable. We differ, though I work for you, in the same company, so I don't dwell on the differences. You come to Brazil; together we shepherd an important shipment through customs. You return to New York and tell your friends at lunch, "I had to pay." They are shocked, or would be if South American customs officials were not so notorious. I have dinner with friends that night, and tell them, "The man didn't want to pay." They are shocked, or would be if North American business practices were not often thought to be so bizarre. Both of us are right, as long as we base our standards on what we believe to be best for society. I think, "Customs agents need the money; our government sets their salary assuming that they make a small percentage"; you think, "The system would work better if everyone were much more honest." Both of our standards are based upon what we believe to be best for our society; consequently both are "right." Now, if we had the time and wanted to make the effort, we could search for a universal principle that would help us define what we meant by "best" for our society, and if we could measure that benefit, then we might be able to agree on which of our standards was more "right." What I am trying to explain, using this illustration, is that two different moral standards can both be *believed* "right"; that is not the same thing as saying that the two different moral standards *are* "right." We have to accept the proposition that we bear some responsibility for other members of our society or life becomes very "solitary, nasty, brutish, and short," for us as well as for others. That responsibility becomes the absolute upon which our ethical systems are based.

This is somewhat in the nature of an aside, but the question of moral relativism—whether moral standards are valid across groups and cultures and times, or whether moral standards just depend upon individual and social and cultural circumstances— is sometimes applied to business firms. It is possible to think of business as a "game" in which different rules apply than in everyday life—a game similar to poker or dice in which no one expects the truth to be fully spoken or contracts to be fully honored.[2] Game strategy, it is said, requires exaggerations and concealments in making statements; the hearer has to be vigilant. Game outcome, it is alleged, encourages shortfalls in fulfilling contracts; the buyer has to be wary.

It is not difficult to find evidence of this "game" approach to business. Company-union wage negotiations are seldom examples of verisimilitude. Public accountants would not be needed if all financial figures were accurately reported. There is a reason that gas pumps and grocery scales are inspected by a public agency and sealed to prevent tampering.

What do you think of this view of management as a game, in which almost any act is permitted that the other side does not detect and offset, a game in which the rules are set by the players, using their moral standards, which are "fully as good as anyone else's"? How would you argue against this view? You should come back to the absolute of some responsibility for other members of society, which has been exhibited by every other culture at every other time, and you set the rule that their moral standards *that benefit society* are fully as good as anyone else's that benefit society. The standards of lying and cheating benefit only the liar and the cheater; if those standards are applied to everyone, the advantages disappear, and society becomes impossible, with no truth and no trust.

Given that you accept the basic premise that both you and I bear some form of responsibility for other people within our society, and that our society cannot continue to exist without some standards of behavior between individuals and groups, how do we determine whether those standards are "right" or "wrong"? We all have an intuitive understanding of right and wrong, but we don't know exactly how to classify our own actions, or those of our neighbors.

The universal recognition that we owe something to other people within our society, and that we are bound by a concept of right and wrong in our behavior to those people, has to be made operational. That is, we have to establish some consistent analytical method to classify our actions as "right" or "wrong." If we can't, it's not for lack of trying. As mentioned before, intellectual history over the past 2,400 years has been filled with attempts to justify moral standards and to establish ethical systems. None work perfectly, but there are five major systems that do have a direct relevance to managerial decisions: Eternal Law, Utilitarian Theory, Universalist Theory, Distributive Justice, and Personal Liberty.

ETERNAL LAW

Many church leaders and some philosophers (Thomas Aquinas and Thomas Jefferson among them) believe that there is an Eternal Law, incorporated in the mind of God, apparent in the state of Nature, revealed in the Holy Scripture, and immediately obvious to any man or woman who will take the time to study either nature or the Scripture. Thomas Jefferson, really the first of the secular humanists, believed that the truths of this law were "self-evident," in his famous phrase, that the rights were "inalienable," and that the duties could easily be derived from the rights. If people had rights to "life, liberty and the pursuit of happiness," then they had obligations to ensure those rights to others, even if this meant revolution against the British Crown. Religious leaders tend to emphasize the revealed source of the truth more than the reasoned nature, but they also believe that the state of the Law is unchanging, and that the rights and duties are obvious: if we are Loved, then we must love others.[3] This reciprocal exchange is summarized in Christian theology by the Golden Rule: Do unto others as you would have others do unto you.

What is wrong with Eternal Law or Natural Law, interpreted by either religious leaders or normative philosophers, as the basis for an ethical system in management? Nothing, except for the number of interpretations. No two Natural Law theorists, and very few religious writers, have ever been able to agree on the exact provisions of the revealed or reasoned truth. Each religion provides moral standards for their members, and many of the members observe those standards in daily life, but the standards differ between groups, and there is no way to determine which one is "right" or "best" or "proper" for the full society. Even the Golden Rule, that simple, elegant, sensible guide to life, can't somehow be applied universally. If you were a wealthy person, you would probably want others to retain their wealth, and you would expect to be treated the same way. If I were a poor person, I would wish others to share their income and benefits, just as I would be willing to share the little I had. Religious rules of conduct tend to be situation dependent; that is, our interpretation of them seems to vary with our personal circumstances. This may happen because most of our religious injunctions for moral behavior were developed many years ago in an agricultural society that had greater equality between individuals but less liberty for each person; the rules are not easily applied in an industrial society with those conditions exactly reversed.

UTILITARIANISM: A TELEOLOGICAL THEORY

The teleological approach to managerial ethics places complete emphasis upon the outcome, not the intent, of individual actions. Teleology is derived from a Greek term that means outcome or result, and some of the most influential philosphers in the Western tradition—including Jeremy Bentham and J. S. Mill—have held that the moral worth of personal conduct can be determined solely by the consequences of that behavior. That is, an act or decision is "right" if it results in benefits for people, and it is "wrong" if it leads to damages or harm; the objective obviously is to create the greatest degree of benefits for the largest number of people while incurring the least amount of damages or harm.

The benefits can vary. Material benefits are not the only ones that count, though they are certainly a good starting place for the calculations, but friendships, knowledge, health, and the other satisfactions we all find in life should be included as well. Think in terms of satisfactions, not pleasures; focusing on pleasures can lead to a very hedonistic and self-centered approach. The aggregate satisfactions or benefits for everyone within society have to be considered.

The benefits are not all positive. There are negative costs and adverse outcomes associated with each action, and they have to be included to establish a balance. The negative costs and adverse outcomes include pain, sickness, death, ignorance, isolation, and unhappiness. The aggregate harms or costs have to be considered, and then a balance of the net consequences can be computed.

This teleological ethical system—focusing on net consequences not individual intentions—is termed Utilitarianism, a philosophy originated by Jeremy Bentham (1748–1832), a British thinker. The name of the philosophy is derived from the word *utility*, which had an eighteenth-century meaning that referred to the degree of usefulness of a household object or a domestic animal; that is, a horse could be said to have a utility for plowing beyond the cost of its upkeep. *Utility* has this same meaning, and this same derivation, in microeconomic theory; it measures our degree of preference for a given good or service relative to price. In Utilitarian theory, the term refers to our perception of the net benefits and costs associated with a given act.

Utilitarianism is obviously close to the economic concept of cost/benefit analysis, particularly as the benefits are not to be confused with expediency and have to be calculated for the long-term consequences as carefully as for the short-term outcomes. Utilities, both benefits and costs, have to be computed equally for everyone. My satisfactions, and my costs, cannot be considered to be more important in some way than your satisfactions, and your costs. The decision rule that is then followed is to produce the greatest net benefits for society; an act is "right" if, and only if, it produces greater net benefits for society than any other act possible under the circumstances. There are of course problems in measuring net benefits—the combination of positive and negative outcomes associated with the act—but mathematical precision is not required; we can approximate the outcomes and include them in our calculations.

Utilitarianism differs from the economic concept of cost/benefit analysis in that the distribution of the costs and benefits has to be included as well. That is, these are net benefits to society, and each individual within the society has to be considered equally, and treated equally in the distribution. "The greatest good for the greatest number" takes precedence in Utilitarian theory over "The greatest good for a smaller, more elite number."

To save time, and to avoid the need to compute the full consequences of every decision and action, most Utilitarians recommend the adoption of simplifying rules. These rules, such as "always tell the truth" or "never renege on a contract," can be logically shown to lead to beneficial outcomes in all foreseeable cases, but the basis for the rules remains the balance of positive and negative consequences that come from every act or decision.

What is wrong with Utilitarianism? Not very much, except for the possibility of exploitation. In the vast majority of cases, where no one is going to be hurt very badly, and particularly where it is possible to use financial equivalents for both the costs and the benefits, it is a familiar and useful form of analysis. But, there is always the possibility of justifying benefits for the great majority of the population by imposing sacrifices or penalties on a small minority. For example, substantial benefits could be brought to large numbers of the American people by expropriating all the property of the readers of the *Harvard Business Review*. This proposal, which might win the approval of a few truly liberal economists and a few extremely opportunistic politicians, would hopefully be rejected by all normative philosophers. Utilitarianism fails because in reality it is two principles: greatest good and greatest number; at some point in our decision processes on important matters, these two principles come into conflict, and then we have no single means of determining what is the "right" or "best" or "proper" act.

Lastly, Utilitarianism fails because we can probably all agree that there are some actions that are simply wrong, despite great apparent net benefits for a huge majority. Doestoevsky provided the extreme example. In the *Brothers Karamazov* he asked what should be done if the happiness of the whole human race, forever, could be brought about by the sacrifice of only one person, one completely innocent child, who would have to be tortured to death. No one should ever be able to accept that exchange. Teleological theory fails as a determinant of moral actions because it is impossible to balance the benefits of the majority against the sacrifices of a minority.

UNIVERSALISM: A DEONTOLOGICAL THEORY

The deontological approach to managerial ethics, in essence, is the reverse of teleological theory. Deontology is derived from another Greek term referring to the duties or the obligations of an individual. This ethical theory states that the moral worth of an action cannot be dependent upon the outcome because those outcomes are so indefinite and uncertain at the time the decision to act is made; instead, the moral worth of an action has to depend upon the intentions of the person making the decision or performing the act. If I wish the best for others, then my moral actions are praiseworthy, even though I happen to be an ineffectual and clumsy individual who always seems to be breaking something or hurting someone. It is assumed that we are not all clumsy and ineffectual people, and therefore that good intentions will normally result in beneficial outcomes.

Personal intentions can be translated into personal duties or obligations because, if we truly wish the best for others, then we will always act in certain ways to ensure beneficial results, and those ways become duties that are incumbent upon us rather than choices that are open to us. It is our duty to tell the truth; it is our duty to adhere to contracts; it is our duty not to take property that belongs to others. (Truthfulness, legality, and honesty can be logically derived from the basic principles of all ethical systems; in deontological theory they are duties we owe to others, while in teleological theory they are the actions that bring the greatest benefits to others.)

Our personal duties are universal, applicable to everyone, and consequently much of deontological theory is also termed Universalism, just as large portions of teleological theory are called Utilitarianism. The first duty of Universalism is to treat others as ends and not as means. Other people should be seen as valuable ends in themselves, worthy of dignity and respect, and not as impersonal means to achieve our own ends. No actions can be considered "right" in accordance with personal duty if it disregards the ultimate moral worth of any other human being.

Immanuel Kant (1724–1804) proposed a simple test for personal duty and goodwill, to eliminate self-interest and self-deception, and to ensure regard for the moral worth of others. The test is to ask yourself whether you would be willing to have everyone in the world, faced with similar circumstances, forced to act in exactly the same way. This is the Categorical Imperative; "categorical," of course, means absolute or unqualified, and the precept is that an act or decision can be judged to be "good" or "right" or "proper" only if everyone must, without qualification, perform the same act or reach the same decision, given similar circumstances.

Kant starts with the simple proposition that it is unfair for me to do something that others don't do or can't do or won't do. This is not because the total effects upon society might be harmful if everyone took the same action such as refusing to pay taxes—that would be a utilitarian doctrine based upon outcomes rather than a universalist precept based upon duties—but because I owe others the duty of acting consistently. I have a "will," or a view of the way I want the world to be, and my views must be consistent or I would have a "contradiction in wills," which is not fair to others given my duty to act rationally and consistently. That is, I pay taxes not because if everyone else did not pay taxes the government would collapse and there would be chaos, but because I want a world of law and order, and therefore I must also want to provide the financial support for that law and order. Law and order and taxes are right for me if, and only if, they are right for everyone else—that is, if they are "universalizable." Kant can be understood as an attempt to tie moral actions to rational decisions, with rationality defined as being based upon consistent and universal maxims. Moral standards, according to Kant, are based upon logical consistency.

The two formulations by Kant—(1) to act only in ways that I would wish all others to act, faced with the same set of circumstances, and (2) always to treat other people with dignity and respect—can be viewed as a single injunction. The first version says that what is morally right for me must be morally right for others. Everyone is of equal value. If this is so, then no person's rights should be subordinated to those of anyone else. If that is so, then we must treat people as free and equal in the pursuit of their interests.

Universalism, particularly when supported by the Categorical Imperative test, is a familiar and useful guide to behavior. The common law is a form of Universalism: Everyone, faced with a just debt, should pay that debt and no one, needing money, should rob banks. Company policies that have a legal or ethical content are usually Universalist: All personnel managers, in considering promotions and pay increases, should include length of service as well as individual ability; and no product manager, in setting prices, should contact competitors or agree to trade constraints.

What is wrong with Universalism? It is a useful method of moral reasoning, but there are no priorities and there are no degrees. I might will law and order to be absolute, with no opposition to the government outside of the formal electoral process, while you might prefer greater personal freedoms. I might will that everyone pay taxes at 7 percent of their annual income, while you might believe that a graduated income tax would be more equitable. Universalism is another ethical system that seems to be very dependent for interpretation upon the situation of the individual. Even the more basic formulation of the Categorical Imperative—to treat each other as moral objects, worthy of respect and dignity—provides very limited help. It is difficult to treat others as ends and not as means all the time, particularly when many serve as means to our personal ends: storekeepers are means of procuring our dinners; customers are means of earning our livelihoods; employees are means of staffing our factories. Both formulations of the Categorical Imperative have to be filled in with the Utilitarian principle—I should want some rule to be a universal law if the consequences of its adoption would be beneficial to others—or with some other values—justice, freedom, etc.—that summarize whole areas of moral conviction. But that principle and those values have to come from outside of the formal Universalist theory.

DISTRIBUTIVE JUSTICE

Neither of the two classical theories, Utilitarianism or Universalism, can be used to judge all moral actions under all circumstances, and consequently two modern ethical systems have been developed, based more upon values than upon principles. The first of these, the theory of Distributive Justice, has been proposed by John Rawls, a member of the Harvard faculty, and is explicitly based upon the primacy of a single value: justice. Justice is felt to be the first virtue of social institutions, as truth is the first virtue of systems of thought. A theory, however useful and complete, has to be rejected or revised if it is found to be untrue; in the same fashion our laws and institutions, no matter how efficient or accepted, must be reformed or abolished if they are unjust.

Professor Rawls proposes that society is an association of individuals who cooperate to advance the good of all. Therefore the society, and the institutions within that society, are marked by conflict as well as by collaboration. The collaboration comes about since individuals recognize that joint actions generate much greater benefits than solitary efforts; the conflict is inherent because people are concerned by the just distribution of those benefits. Each person prefers a greater to a lesser share and proposes a system of distribution to ensure that greater share. These distributive systems can have very different bases: to each person equally, or to each according to his or her need, to his or her effort, to his or her contribution, or to his or her competence. Most modern economic systems make use of all five principles: public education is, theoretically, distributed equally, while welfare payments are on the basis of need, sales commissions on the basis of effort, public honors on the basis of contribution, and managerial salaries on the basis of competence.

Professor Rawls believes that these assorted distributive systems are unjust. He suggests that the primacy of justice in the basic structure of our society requires greater equality, because free and rational persons, recognizing the obvious benefits of cooperation and concerned about the just distribution of those benefits, would accept social and economic inequalities only if they could be shown to result in compensating benefits for everyone, and particularly for the least advantaged members of society: poor, unskilled, and with native intelligence but no training. According to Rawls, I would not object to your having more of the social and economic benefits than I do, but I would object to working hard, beyond the minimum level of effort required to maintain my present standard of living, just so that you could have more. It is not hard to find evidence of this attitude within our society, so the theory of distributive justice does appear to have some empirical support.

Professor Rawls starts, however, not with our societies, but with a "natural state," a hypothetical existence at the beginning of time when people were still ignorant of the exact nature of the differences among them—that is, when no one knew who was the most talented, the most energetic, the most competent. What reciprocal arrangement, he asks, would people under those conditions make for the just distribution of the benefits produced by their cooperation? This is the familiar idea of the social contract, and the basic question is, What principles would free and rational persons, concerned with furthering their own interests yet wishing to maintain their cooperative efforts, adopt as defining the fundamental terms of their association?

They would not select absolute equality in the distribution of benefits, Professor Rawls argues, because they would recognize that some of them would put forth greater efforts, have greater skills, develop greater competences, and so on. They would not agree to absolute inequality based upon effort, skill, or competence because they would not know who among them had those qualities and consequently who among them would receive the greater and the lesser benefits. Instead, they would develop a concept of conditional inequality, where differences in benefits had to be justified, and they would propose a rule that those differences in benefits could be justified only if they could be shown to result in compensating benefits for everyone, and in particular for the least advantaged members of their society. That is, the distribution of income would be unequal, but the inequalities had to work for the benefit of all, and they would work for the benefit of all by helping in some measure the least advantaged, who would then continue to contribute and cooperate.

Distributive Justice can be expanded from an economic system for the distribution of benefits to an ethical system for the evaluation of behavior in that acts can be considered to be "right" and "just" and "proper" if they lead to greater cooperation by members of our society, and "wrong" and "unjust" and "improper" if they lead in the opposite direction. What are the problems with this concept of distributive justice? It is entirely dependent upon an acceptance of the proposition that social cooperation provides the basis for all economic and social benefits; individual effort is downplayed, if not ignored. We all recognize that some organized activities would never take place unless some one individual was willing to take the risks and responsibilities of starting and directing those activities. This individual effort is ignored in Distributive Justice: it forms the basis, however, for the fifth and last ethical system to be discussed.

PERSONAL LIBERTY

The theory of Personal Liberty (this phrase is my own, developed to contrast with Distributive Justice) is an ethical system proposed by Robert Nozick, also currently a member of the Harvard faculty. This system is another based upon the primacy of a single value, rather than a single principle, but that value is liberty rather than justice. Liberty is thought to be the first requirement of society. An institution or law that violates individual liberty, even though it may result in greater happiness and increased benefits for others, has to be rejected as being unjust.

Professor Nozick agrees that society is an association of individuals, and that cooperation between those individuals is necessary for economic gain, but he would argue that the cooperation comes about as a result of the exchange of goods and services. The holdings of each person, in income, wealth, and the other bases of self-respect, are derived from other people in exchange for some good or service, or are received from other people in the form of a gift. An existing pattern of holdings may have come about through application of any of the principles of distribution (to each equally, or to each according to need, effort, contribution, or competence), but those patterns will be changed by transfers, and those transfers, by exchange or gift, can be considered to be "just" as long as they are volun-

	Nature of the Ethical Belief	*Problems in the Ethical System*
Eternal Law	Moral standards are given in an Eternal Law, which is revealed in Scripture or apparent in nature and then interpreted by religious leaders or humanist philosophers; the belief is that everyone should act in accordance with the interpretation.	There are multiple interpretations of the Law, but no method to choose among them beyond human rationality, and human rationality needs an absolute principle or value as the basis for choice.
Utilitarian Theory	Moral standards are applied to the outcome of an action or decision; the principle is that everyone should act to generate the greatest benefits for the largest number of people.	Immoral acts can be justified if they provide substantial benefits for the majority, even at an unbearable cost or harm to the minority; an additional principle or value is needed to balance the benefit-cost equation.
Universalist Theory	Moral standards are applied to the intent of an action or decision; the principle is that everyone should act to ensure that similar decisions would be reached by others, given similar circumstances.	Immoral acts can be justified by persons who are prone to self-deception or self-importance, and there is no scale to judge between "wills"; an additional principle or value is needed to refine the Categorical Imperative concept.
Distributive Justice	Moral standards are based upon the primacy of a single value, which is justice. Everyone should act to ensure a more equitable distribution of benefits, for this promotes individual self-respect, which is essential for social cooperation.	The primacy of the value of justice is dependent upon acceptance of the proposition that an equitable distribution of benefits ensures social cooperation.
Personal Liberty	Moral standards are based upon the primacy of a single value, which is liberty. Everyone should act to ensure greater freedom of choice, for this promotes market exchange, which is essential for social productivity.	The primacy of the value of liberty is dependent upon acceptance of the proposition that a market system of exchange ensures social productivity.

tary. Nonvoluntary exchanges, based upon the use of social force or other coercive means, are unjust.

Personal Liberty can be expanded from essentially a market system for the exchange of holdings to an ethical system for the evaluation of behavior, because individuals must be allowed to make informed choices among alternative courses of action leading towards their own welfare, and these choices are "just" or "right" or "proper" as long as the same opportunities for informed choices are extended to others. Justice depends upon equal opportunities for choice and exchange, not upon equal allocations of wealth and income. What is wrong with this concept of liberty? It is based upon a very narrow definition of liberty that is limited to the negative right not to suffer interference from others; there may also be a positive right to receive some of the benefits enjoyed by others. That is, the right to life is certainly the right not to be killed by your neighbors, but it may also include the right to continue living through access to some minimal level of food, shelter, clothing, and medical assistance. And, it is assumed that the food, shelter, clothing, and medical assistance are produced through personal initiative, not through social cooperation.

CONCLUSIONS ON NORMATIVE PHILOSOPHY AS THE BASIS FOR MORAL CHOICE

There are five major ethical systems, as summarized in Exhibit 4–1. They do not outwardly conflict with each other—an action such as lying that is considered immoral in one system will generally be considered immoral in all the other systems—but they cannot be reconciled into a logically consistent whole, for eventually conflict will arise over the primacy of the alternative principles and values. Each ethical system expresses a portion of the truth. Each system has adherents and opponents. And each, it is important to admit, is incomplete or inadequate as a means of judging the moral content of individual actions or decisions. What does this mean to managers? I would suggest that there is one major implication for managers, and three more minor or indirect consequences for organizations, that come from the incomplete nature of ethical systems.

The major implication for managers is that there is no single system of belief, with rationally derived standards of moral behavior or methods of moral reasoning, that can guide executives fully in reaching difficult ethical decisions. An ethical decision, to repeat the earlier definition and sharpen the present discussion, is one that will affect others in ways that are beyond their control. A decision to introduce a new brand of chocolate cake mix has no ethical dimensions since others within the society are perfectly free to buy or ignore the product. But a decision to close the plant producing the cake mix, or to use a high-cholesterol shortening in the production of that mix, or to ask for government help in shutting off imports, would have an ethical content, since these issues do have an impact upon others. A product manager, faced let us say in an unlikely but perhaps not totally unrealistic problem with imported cake mixes from a foreign country that has very low wage rates and very high government subsidies, has to respond, and each response has ethical implications. Lowering production means cutting employment; reducing the cost means compromising the quality; and requesting government help means endorsing trade restrictions.

There is no single system of belief to guide managers in reaching difficult ethical decisions, but this does not mean that all of us are on our own, to do as we like in our decisions and actions that affect others. We do have obligations to others. We cannot ignore those obligations. The difficulty comes in identifying our obligations and then in evaluating our alternatives, with no single set of moral standards to guide us.

What should we do? Instead of using just one ethical system, which we must admit is imperfect, we have to use all five systems and think through the consequences of our actions on multiple dimensions. Does a given decision result in greater benefits than damages for society as a whole, not just for our organization as part of that society? Is the decision self-serving, or would we be willing to have everyone else take the same action when faced with the same circumstances? We understand the need for social cooperation; will our decision increase or decrease the willingness of others to contribute? We recognize the importance of personal freedom; will our decision increase or decrease the liberty of others to act? Lastly, we know that the universe is large and infinite, while we are small and our lives are short; is our personal improvement that important, measured against the immensity of that other scale?[4]

Moral reasoning of this nature, utilizing all five ethical systems, is not simple and easy, but it is satisfying. It does work. It works particularly well when combined with economic and legal analysis. That combination will be the topic of the next chapter, Managerial Ethics and Individual Decisions.

Footnotes

I should like to acknowledge the valued support of the Levi Strauss Foundation for the study of managerial ethics during the 1981–82 academic year, and the thoughtful help of Professor Lisa Newton, Department of Philosophy, Fairfield University, in the preparation of this chapter.

1. For a more complete discussion of the very basic question of ethical relativism, see Richard Brand, *Ethical Theory* (New York: Prentice-Hall, 1959).

2. Albert Carr, in a controversial article ("Is Business Bluffing Ethical?" *Harvard Business Review,* January-February 1968) suggested that business is a game, and that it is necessary only to follow the rules of the game, not personal moral standards.

3. It seems awkward to discuss the philosophic basis of religious belief in a book on management, but religious beliefs do have an impact upon managers as well as upon others and should be included in any description of ethical systems.

4. Once again I am faced with the problem of discussing religious beliefs in a book on management, with the added complexity of recognizing that these beliefs differ among the major religious groups in the United States. Rather than use the moral standards of one group as representative of all others, I prefer to refer to the immensity of the concept of an Eternal Law and let each faith infer its own standards based upon an interpretation of that law.

CASES

Seven Ethical Problems for Moral Reasoning

There are, as was described in the text, four major secular systems of ethical belief or methods of normative philosophy that can be used in moral reasoning. The fifth major system, Eternal Law, can certainly be used, but it is pious, not secular, and requires the adoption of a specific religious point of view. You will find, if you have not already observed this, that there is little agreement on religious orthodoxy and that consequently your arguments, while important to you, may have no weight for others. I suggest that you focus, in your analysis, on the four secular systems or methods that are summarized very briefly below:

1. Utilitarianism states that it is the outcome of a decision or action that is important, for it is results that truly matter in our treatment of other people. The principle to be followed is that of beneficiency: a decision or act is right and proper and good only if it generates the greatest amount of benefit for the largest number of people at the lowest cost or harm to others.

2. Universalism states that it is the intent of a decision or action that is important, for we can never accurately foresee and evaluate all the possible results. The principle to be followed is that of consistency: a decision or act is right and proper and good only if we could will that everyone, faced with the same set of circumstances, should be expected to make the same decision or take the same act.

3. Distributive Justice is based upon the primacy of a single value, rather than a single principle, and that value is justice. A belief in the primacy of justice leads us to select decisions and actions as right and proper and good only if the least advantaged members of our society somehow enjoy a better standard of living after the decision or act than they did before.

4. Personal Liberty is also based upon the primacy of a single value rather than a single principle, and in this case that value is liberty. A belief in the primacy of liberty leads us to select decisions and actions as right and proper and good only if all members of our society somehow have a greater freedom to develop their own lives after the decision or act than they did before.

Exercises. Here are seven short ethical problems. Apply the four methods of ethical analysis to each, to see if those methods of moral reasoning help your personal understanding and your eventual decision.

1. *The sale of radar detectors.* Radar detectors, also known as "fuzzbusters," are simple but extremely sensitive radio receivers that are tuned to the wavelength of the police radar. When a car equipped with a detector first enters the radar field, a warning light flashes or a buzzer sounds, enabling the driver to slow down, if necessary, before the speed of the car can be calculated by the police equipment. The use of radar detectors is illegal in most states, but the manufacturing and marketing of the units have never been banned. Question: Should companies make and sell radar detectors?

2. *The size of executive payments.* In 1983, Philip Caldwell, chairman of the Ford Motor Company, received a salary of $1,420,534 and a bonus, primarily through the sale of stock options, of $5,892,024. In that same year, Roger Smith, chairman of General Motors, received a salary and bonus totaling $1,490,490, plus additional stock options that were not disclosed. That same year, 5,807 senior executives at General Motors shared a total cash bonus of $181,705,344. Owen Bieber, president of the United Auto Workers, called those payments "obscene" and cited the fact that many members of his union were still on indefinite layoff from the severe auto recession of 1980 to 1982. Question: Should companies pay large bonuses to senior executives?

3. *The sale of cigarettes in Third World countries.* Cigarette sales have been declining in the United States and Western Europe since 1978, due to the personal concerns of most consumers about health and the legal prohibitions of most governments against advertising. Many cigarette companies, consequently, have turned to Third World countries, using "image" advertising, widespread distribution, and simplified pricing to increase volume. The advertising inevitably depicts successful members of the dominant racial or ethnic group, smoking cigarettes, in enjoyable and enviable surroundings. The distribution is through local shops and markets, to make cigarettes readily available. The pricing is not by the pack but by the single cigarette, to make them easily affordable. The result has been substantial increases in sales. Philip Morris, for example, has increased its international sales over 5 percent each year for the past five years and now sells cigarettes in 170 countries. Question: Should cigarette companies promote the use of their product abroad?

4. *The buyout of public companies.* It has become common over the past few years for the managers of a company to offer to purchase 100 percent of the stock from the shareholders. This is known as "taking the firm private," for it ends the public sale of stock and means that the profits, and the risks, will be concentrated in a small, new group of owners. Financing for the purchase is usually generated by investment bankers, who receive part of the equity in exchange for providing a large, highly leveraged loan secured by the assets of the purchased firm. The original shareholders are not forced to sell, but by definition they know less than the management about the true value and future potential of the firm and consequently have to rely on the assertions of the managers and investment bankers to gauge whether the price that is offered for their shares is adequate. Question: Should corporate managers and investment bankers purchase private control of public companies?

5. *The diversification of U.S. Steel.* The U.S. Steel Company was, at one time, the largest and most profitable of all steel firms, on a global

basis. From the end of World War II, in 1945, until the advent of low-cost imports from developing countries in 1977, the company was the leader in tonnage, technology, and profitability; earnings during that period never dropped below a 17 percent return on equity. Earnings after 1977, however, deteriorated rapidly, averaging less than 3 percent on equity for the next seven years. Senior executives decided that the company had to diversify, and in 1983 Marathon Oil Company was purchased for $5.93 billion, followed by Husky Oil Company for $488 million in 1984, and Texas Oil and Gas, for $3.03 billion, in 1985. Oil and gas accounted, in 1985, for 53 percent of the revenues and 81 percent of the profits. However, many residents of the steel-producing regions of Pennsylvania and Ohio, and many former employees of the company, felt that the expenditures to acquire the oil companies had been improper. They pointed out that the $9.6 billion spent for diversification would have paid for two completely modern steel mills, able to compete on a cost and quality basis with any foreign producer. Question: Should the U.S. Steel Company have diversified out of its basic business into the oil industry, given the adverse consequences on employment and economic development in the original communities?

6. *The influence of Political Action Committees.* In 1974, after investigation of charges that both unions and corporations had made secret contributions to the 1972 presidential campaign, Congress passed a comprehensive campaign-finance law. This law provided public financing for presidential elections and placed limits on the amounts that could be contributed to congressional candidates by both individuals and organizations. However, associations of individuals and organizations were not prohibited from spending additional funds, either in direct contributions or in indirect support through advertising, rallies, and so on. These associations, generally with a distinct industrial or ideological orientation—e.g., Realtors, lumber producers, auto workers, or advocates of a strong defense—have become known as Political Action Committees, or PACs. The number of PACs has expanded rapidly, from less than 600 in 1974 to over 4,200 in 1984. The amount of money they contribute, both directly and indirectly to congressional candidates, has also grown rapidly, to $113 million in 1984 (split, surprisingly, $64 million for Democratic candidates and $49 million for the Republicans). Question: Should individuals, whether in corporations, unions, or special interest groups, contribute to congressional campaigns through Political Action Committees?

7. *The consequences of malpractice suits.* In 1975 there were 5 malpractice claims for every 100 doctors; by 1983 the number had risen to 16

for every 100. The average award or settlement in 1975 was $26,000; by 1983 the amount had risen to $330,000. The average award in some populous sections of the country, such as California and New York City, had grown to $650,000. Malpractice insurance, in 1983, cost $55,000 a year for an obstetrician on Long Island and over $100,000 a year for a neurosurgeon in California. Total annual premiums for malpractice insurance within the United States are $2 billion currently (1985), and physicians allege that they prescribe over $15 billion in unnecessary tests as part of "defensive medicine." Attorneys respond that the principle of tort law, under which medical malpractice claims are tried, is that a "victim should be made whole." The victim of an inaccurate diagnosis or botched operation can't be "made whole" physically, and so money is paid instead.

Physicians are not the only ones who have been sued; many drug companies have also. In 1985, Lederle Labs, the sole manufacturer of whooping cough vaccine, said that it would stop production the following year because of 150 medical liability cases charging that the vaccine caused brain damage. The company believes that there is no scientific evidence of a connection between the vaccine and brain damage, citing numerous government health lab and university and corporate studies, but juries have awarded large damages in 2 cases; 84 resulted in verdicts for the company, and 64 others are pending. Whooping cough at one time was one of the most serious childhood illnesses, always debilitating and sometimes life-threatening. The incidence of the illness now is very low, due to the widespread use of the vaccine, but Lederle Labs is the last of the manufacturers; three others stopped production earlier due to the lawsuits and liability claims. Question: Should Lederle Labs continue the production of whooping cough vaccine?

The Parable of the Sadhu

Last year, as the first participant in the new six-month sabbatical program that Morgan Stanley has adopted, I enjoyed a rare opportunity to collect my thoughts as well as do some traveling. I spent the first three months in Nepal, walking 600 miles through 200 villages in the Himalayas and climbing some 120,000 vertical feet. On the trip my sole Western companion was an anthropologist who shed light on the cultural patterns of the villages we passed through.

During the Nepal hike, something occurred that has had a powerful impact on my thinking about corporate ethics. Although some might argue that the experience has no relevance to business, it was a situation in which a basic ethical dilemma suddenly intruded into the lives of a group of individuals. How the group responded I think holds a lesson for all organizations no matter how defined.

SOURCE: Bowen H. McCoy, reprinted from *Harvard Business Review,* September-October 1983. Copyright © 1983 by the President and Fellows of Harvard College.

The Sadhu

The Nepal experience was more rugged and adventuresome than I had anticipated. Most commercial treks last two or three weeks and cover a quarter of the distance we traveled.

My friend Stephen, the anthropologist, and I were halfway through the 60-day Himalayan part of the trip when we reached the high point, an 18,000-foot pass over a crest that we'd have to traverse to reach to the village of Muklinath, an ancient holy place for pilgrims.

Six years earlier I had suffered pulmonary edema, an acute form of altitude sickness, at 16,500 feet in the vicinity of Everest base camp, so we were understandably concerned about what would happen at 18,000 feet. Moreover, the Himalayas were having their wettest spring in 20 years; hip-deep powder and ice had already driven us off one ridge. If we failed to cross the pass, I feared that the last half of our "once in a lifetime" trip would be ruined.

The night before we would try the pass, we camped at a hut at 14,500 feet. In the photos taken at that camp, my face appears wan. The last village we'd passed through was a sturdy two-day walk below us, and I was tired.

During the late afternoon, four backpackers from New Zealand joined us, and we spent most of the night awake, anticipating the climb. Below we could see the fires of two other parties, which turned out to be two Swiss couples and a Japanese hiking club.

To get over the steep part of the climb before the sun melted the steps cut in the ice, we departed at 3:30 A.M. The New Zealanders left first, followed by Stephen and myself, our porters and Sherpas, and then the Swiss. The Japanese lingered in their camp. The sky was clear, and we were confident that no spring storm would erupt that day to close the pass.

At 15,500 feet, it looked to me as if Stephen were shuffling and staggering a bit, which are symptoms of altitude sickness. (The initial stage of altitude sickness brings a headache and nausea. As the condition worsens, a climber may encounter difficult breathing, disorientation, aphasia, and paralysis.) I felt strong, my adrenaline was flowing, but I was very concerned about my ultimate ability to get across. A couple of our porters were also suffering from the height, and Pasang, our Sherpa sirdar (leader), was worried.

Just after daybreak, while we rested at 15,500 feet, one of the New Zealanders, who had gone ahead, came staggering down toward us with a body slung across his shoulders. He dumped the almost naked, barefoot body of an Indian holy man—a sadhu—at my feet. He had found the pilgrim lying on the ice, shivering and suffering from hypothermia. I cradled the sadhu's head and laid him out on the rocks. The New Zealander was angry. He wanted to get across the pass before the bright sun melted the snow. He said, "Look, I've done what I can. You have porters and Sherpa guides. You care for him. We're going on!" He turned and went back up the mountain to join his friends.

I took a carotid pulse and found that the sadhu was still alive. We figured he had probably visited the holy shrines at Muklinath and was on his way home. It was fruitless to question why he had chosen this desperately high route instead of the safe, heavily traveled caravan route through the Kali Gandaki gorge. Or why he was almost naked and with no shoes, or how long he had been lying in the pass. The answers weren't going to solve our problem.

Stephen and the four Swiss began stripping off outer clothing and opening their packs. The sadhu was soon clothed from head to foot. He was not able to walk, but he was very much alive. I looked down the mountain and spotted below the Japanese climbers marching up with a horse.

Without a great deal of thought, I told Stephen and Pasang

that I was concerned about withstanding the heights to come and wanted to get over the pass. I took off after several of our porters who had gone ahead.

On the steep part of the ascent where, if the ice steps had given way, I would have slid down about 3,000 feet, I felt vertigo. I stopped for a breather, allowing the Swiss to catch up with me. I inquired about the sadhu and Stephen. They said that the sadhu was fine and that Stephen was just behind. I set off again for the summit.

Stephen arrived at the summit an hour after I did. Still exhilarated by victory, I ran down the snow slope to congratulate him. He was suffering from altitude sickness, walking 15 steps, then stopping, walking 15 steps, then stopping. Pasang accompanied him all the way up. When I reached them, Stephen glared at me and said: "How do you feel about contributing to the death of a fellow man?"

I did not fully comprehend what he meant.

"Is the sadhu dead?" I inquired.

"No," replied Stephen, "but he surely will be!"

After I had gone, and the Swiss had departed not long after, Stephen had remained with the sadhu. When the Japanese had arrived, Stephen had asked to use their horse to transport the sadhu down to the hut. They had refused. He had then asked Pasang to have a group of our porters carry the sadhu. Pasang had resisted the idea, saying that the porters would have to exert all their energy to get themselves over the pass. He had thought they could not carry a man down 1,000 feet to the hut, reclimb the slope, and get across safely before the snow melted. Pasang had pressed Stephen not to delay any longer.

The Sherpas had carried the sadhu down to a rock in the sun at about 15,000 feet and had pointed out the hut another 500 feet below. The Japanese had given him food and drink. When they had last seen him he was listlessly throwing rocks at the Japanese party's dog, which had frightened him.

We do not know if the sadhu lived or died.

For many of the following days and evenings Stephen and I discussed and debated our behavior toward the sadhu. Stephen is a committed Quaker with deep moral vision. He said, "I feel that what happened with the sadhu is a good example of the breakdown between the individual ethic and the corporate ethic. No one person was willing to assume ultimate responsibility for the sadhu. Each was willing to do his bit just so long as it was not too inconvenient. When it got to be a bother, everyone just passed the buck to someone else and took off. Jesus was relevant to a more individualistic stage of society, but how do we interpret his teaching today in a world filled with large, impersonal organizations and groups?"

I defended the larger group, saying, "Look, we all cared. We all stopped and gave aid and comfort. Everyone did his bit. The New Zealander carried him down below the snow line. I took his pulse and suggested we treat him for hypothermia. You and the Swiss gave him clothing and got him warmed up. The Japanese gave him food and water. The Sherpas carried him down to the sun and pointed out the easy trail toward the hut. He was well enough to throw rocks at a dog. What more could we do?"

"You have just described the typical affluent Westerner's response to a problem. Throwing money—in this case food and sweaters—at it, but not solving the fundamentals!" Stephen retorted.

"What would satisfy you?" I said. "Here we are, a group of New Zealanders, Swiss, Americans, and Japanese who have never met before and who are at the apex of one of the most powerful experiences of our lives. Some years the pass is so bad no one gets over it. What right does an almost naked pilgrim who chooses the wrong trail have to disrupt our lives? Even the Sherpas had no interest in risking the trip to help him beyond a certain point."

Stephen calmly rebutted, "I wonder what the Sherpas would have done if the sadhu had been a well-dressed Nepali, or what the Japanese would have done if the sadhu had been a well-dressed Asian, or what you would have done, Buzz, if the sadhu had been a well-dressed Western woman?"

"Where, in your opinion," I asked instead, "is the limit of our responsibility in a situation like this? We had our own well-being to worry about. Our Sherpa guides were unwilling to jeopardize us or the porters for the sadhu. No one else on the mountain was willing to commit himself beyond certain self-imposed limits."

Stephen said, "As individual Christians or people with a Western ethical tradition, we can fulfill our obligations in such a situation only if (1) the sadhu dies in our care, (2) the sadhu demonstrates to us that he could undertake the two-day walk down to the village, or (3) we carry the sadhu for two days down to the village and convince someone there to care for him."

"Leaving the sadhu in the sun with food and clothing, while he demonstated hand-eye coordination by throwing a rock at a dog, comes close to fulfilling items one and two," I answered. "And it wouldn't have made sense to take him to the village where the people appeared to be far less caring than the Sherpas, so the third condition is impractical. Are you really saying that, no matter what the implications, we should, at the drop of a hat, have changed our entire plan?"

The Individual vs. the Group Ethic

Despite my arguments, I felt and continue to feel guilt about the sadhu. I had literally walked through a classic moral dilemma without fully thinking through the consequences. My excuses for my actions include a high adrenaline flow, a superordinate goal, and a once-in-a-lifetime opportunity—factors in the usual corporate situation, especially when one is under stress.

Real moral dilemmas are ambiguous, and many of us hike right through them, unaware that they exist. When, usually after the fact, someone makes an issue of them, we tend to resent his or her bringing it up. Often, when the full import of what we have done (or not done) falls on us, we dig into a defensive position from which it is very difficult to emerge. In rare circumstances we may contemplate what we have done from inside a prison.

Had we mountaineers been free of physical and mental stress caused by the effort and the high altitude, we might have treated the sadhu differently. Yet isn't stress the real test of personal and corporate values? The instant decisions executives make under pressure reveal the most about personal and corporate character.

Among the many questions that occur to me when pondering my experience are: What are the practical limits of moral imagination and vision? Is there a collective or institutional ethic beyond the ethics of the individual? At what level of effort or commitment can one discharge one's ethical responsibilities?

Not every ethical dilemma has a right solution. Reasonable people often disagree; otherwise there would be no dilemma. In a business context, however, it is essential that managers agree on a process for dealing with dilemmas.

The sadhu experience offers an interesting parallel to business situations. An immediate response was mandatory. Failure to act was a decision in itself. Up on the mountain we could not resign and submit our résumés to a headhunter. In contrast to philosophy, business involves action and implementation—getting things done. Managers must come up with answers to problems based on what they see and what they allow to influence their decision-making processes. On the mountain, none of us but Stephen realized the true dimensions of the situation we were facing.

One of our problems was that as a group we had no process for developing a consensus. We had no sense of purpose or plan. The difficulties of dealing with the sadhu were so complex that no one person could handle it. Because it did not have a set of preconditions that could guide its action to an acceptable resolution, the group reacted instinctively as individuals. The cross-cultural nature of the group added a further layer of complexity. We had no leader with whom we could all identify and in whose purpose we believed. Only Stephen was willing to take charge, but he could not gain adequate support to care for the sadhu.

Some organizations do have a value system that transcends the personal values of the managers. Such values, which go beyond profitability, are usually revealed when the organization is under stress. People throughout the organization generally accept its values, which, because they are not presented as a rigid list of commandments, may be somewhat ambiguous. The stories people tell, rather than printed materials, transmit these conceptions of what is proper behavior.

For 20 years I have been exposed at senior levels to a variety of corporations and organizations. It is amazing how quickly an outsider can sense the tone and style of an organization and the degree of tolerated openness and freedom to challenge management.

Organizations that do not have a heritage of mutually accepted, shared values tend to become unhinged during stress, with each individual bailing out for himself. In the great takeover battles we have witnessed during past years, companies that had strong cultures drew the wagons around them and fought it out, while other companies saw executives, supported by their golden parachutes, bail out of the struggles.

Because corporations and their members are interdependent, for the corporation to be strong the members need to share a preconceived notion of what is correct behavior, a "business ethic," and think of it as a positive force, not a constraint.

As an investment banker I am continually warned by well-meaning lawyers, clients, and associates to be wary of conflicts of interest. Yet if I were to run away from every difficult situation, I wouldn't be an effective investment banker. I have to feel my way through conflicts. An effective manager can't run from risk either; he or she has to confront and deal with risk. To feel "safe" in doing this, managers need the guidelines of an agreed-on process and set of values within the organization.

After my three months in Nepal, I spent three months as an executive-in-residence at both Stanford Business School and the Center for Ethics and Social Policy at the Graduate Theological Union at Berkeley. These six months away from my job gave me time to assimilate 20 years of business experience. My thoughts turned often to the meaning of the leadership role in any large organization. Students at the seminary thought of themselves as antibusiness. But when I questioned them they agreed that they distrusted all large organizations, including the church. They perceived all large organizations as impersonal and opposed to individual values and needs. Yet we all know of organizations where peoples' values and beliefs are respected and their expressions encouraged. What makes the difference? Can we identify the difference and, as a result, manage more effectively?

The word "ethics" turns off many and confuses more. Yet the notions of shared values and an agreed-on process for dealing with adversity and change—what many people mean when they talk about corporate culture—seem to be at the heart of the ethical issue. People who are in touch with their own core beliefs and the beliefs of others and are sustained by them can be more comfortable living on the cutting edge. At times, taking a tough line or a decisive stand in a muddle of ambiguity is the only ethical thing to do. If a manager is indecisive and spends time trying to figure out the "good" thing to do, the enterprise may be lost.

Business ethics, then, has to do with the authenticity and integrity of the enterprise. To be ethical is to follow the business as well as the cultural goals of the corporation, its owners, its employees, and its customers. Those who cannot serve the corporate vision are not authentic business people and, therefore, are not ethical in the business sense.

At this stage of my own business experience I have a strong interest in organizational behavior. Sociologists are keenly studying what they call corporate stories, legends, and heroes as a way organizations have of transmitting the value system. Corporations such as Arco have even hired consultants to perform an audit of their corporate culture. In a company, the leader is the person who understands, interprets, and manages the corporate value system. Effective managers are then action-oriented people who resolve conflict, are tolerant of ambiguity, stress, and change, and have a strong sense of purpose for themselves and their organizations.

If all this is true, I wonder about the role of the professional manager who moves from company to company. How can he or she quickly absorb the values and culture of different organizations? Or is there, indeed, an art of management that is totally transportable? Assuming such fungible managers do exist, is it proper for them to manipulate the values of others?

What would have happened had Stephen and I carried the sadhu for two days back to the village and become involved with the villagers in his care? In four trips to Nepal my most interesting experiences occurred in 1975 when I lived in a Sherpa home in the Khumbu for five days recovering from altitude sickness. The high point of Stephen's trip was an invitation to participate in a family funeral ceremony in Manang. Neither experience had to do with climbing the high passes of the Himalayas. Why were we so reluctant to try the lower path, the ambiguous trail? Perhaps because we did not have a leader who could reveal the greater purpose of the trip to us.

Why didn't Stephen with his moral vision opt to take the sadhu under his personal care? The answer is because, in part, Stephen was hard-stressed physically himself, and because, in part, without some support system that involved our involuntary and episodic community on the mountain, it was beyond his individual capacity to do so.

I see the current interest in corporate culture and corporate value systems as a positive response to Stephen's pessimism about the decline of the role of the individual in large organizations. Individuals who operate from a thoughtful set of personal values provide the foundation for a corporate culture. A corporate tradition that encourages freedom of inquiry, supports personal values, and reinforces a focused sense of direction can fulfill the need for individuality along with the prosperity and success of the group. Without such corporate support, the individual is lost.

That is the lesson of the sadhu. In a complex corporate situation, the individual requires and deserves the support of the group. If people cannot find such support from their organization, they don't know how to act. If such support is forthcoming, a person has a stake in the success of the group, and can add much to the process of establishing and maintaining a corporate culture. It is management's challenge to be sensitive to individual needs, to shape them, and to direct and focus them for the benefit of the group as a whole.

For each of us the sadhu lives. Should we stop what we are doing and comfort him; or should we keep trudging up toward the high pass? Should I pause to help the derelict I pass on the street each night as I walk by the Yale club en route to Grand Central Station? Am I his brother? What is the nature of our responsibility if we consider ourselves to be ethical persons? Perhaps it is to change the values of the group so that it can, with all its resources, take the other road.

CHAPTER 5

Managerial Ethics and Individual Decisions

We have looked at economic analysis, legal analysis, and philosophical analysis as means of resolving ethical dilemmas and
have found that none is completely satisfactory. When we must
attempt to find a balance between the economic and the social
performance of an organization, none gives us a method of de-
ciding upon a course of action that we can say with certainty is
"right" and "proper" and "good."

Economic analysis was the first to be investigated. Aiming
toward Pareto Optimality by means of impersonal market forces
is appealing—all we have to do, then, is to maximize revenues
and minimize costs, and the product markets, factor markets,
and political decisions will together eliminate or correct the harm
or damages we cause to others. However, there are both practical
and theoretical problems with microeconomic theory. We have to
admit that markets are not that efficient and that voters are not
that generous.

Legal analysis was the next to be considered. The concept of
impersonal social processes is also appealing—all we have to do
is to obey the law and we can feel that we are meeting the collective moral standards of a majority of our population. However,
that concept falls apart as we look at the process by which individual norms, beliefs, and values are institutionalized into the
legal framework. We have to recognize that there are too many
steps, and too many compromises, between individual moral
standards and national legal requirements.

Philosophical analysis was the last to be reviewed. The concept of personal rational analysis is appealing—all we have to do is base our decisions upon a single principle (beneficiency or consistency) or upon a single value (justice or freedom)—but rational analysis has an internal flaw. If we attempt to use any one of the principles or any one of the values in moral reasoning, we find that we have to add a second principle or a second value to reach a logical conclusion. We have to accept that a combination of conflicting principles or values is not rational.

What do we do, then? How do we decide, when faced with an ethical dilemma that contrasts economic performance and social performance? We are forced to use all three methods of analysis.

We are forced to say to ourselves that if one of our decisions or actions generates an adequate financial return, conforms to current law, provides substantial benefits to a large number of people, is an action we can wish that everyone else would take faced with the same set of alternatives and background factors, is "just" in the sense of increasing the potential for social cooperation, and is "equitable" in the sense of expanding the ability of others to choose for themselves—then we can say that decision or action is "right" and "proper" and "good."

Granted, this form of multiple analysis is complex. It would be better if we had a single decision rule that we could follow every time, but we don't. Does multiple analysis work? Yes, I think that it does. Let me show that it does by following through two examples of foreign bribery, one of which I think most of us would agree to be "wrong" and the other of which I think most of us would agree to be "permissible" if not "right." We will see whether multiple analysis helps us to understand our intuitive beliefs—based upon our personal moral standards—when confronting a reasonably simple ethical problem, then I think that we can place greater reliance upon it when we don't have clear intuitive feelings and we face much more complex ethical issues.

ETHICAL ANALYSIS AND THE LOCKHEED BRIBERY CASE

The first example—and the one that I think we can agree to be intuitively "wrong"—is that of the Lockheed Aircraft Corporation, which paid $3.8 million to various governmental officials and representatives of the prime minister in Japan to ensure the purchase of 20 TriStar passenger planes. This event was extensively reported, following testimony before a congressional investigating committee, and Carl Kotchian, the president of Lockheed, has written an account of the conditions that led him to decide to pay the bribes. In his defense, I think that we have to understand that Mr. Kotchian did not leave for Japan carrying the corporate checkbook and a ballpoint pen; in essence he was forced into the payments.

Carl Kotchian was directly responsible for the negotiations that led to the sale of the TriStar planes. However, he did not speak Japanese and had to rely on advice and representations from the executives of a Japanese trading company that had been retained to act as the agent for Lockheed. I think that we can assume that Mr. Kotchian had been prepared by his staff for the personal nature of Japanese business decisions on large-scale investments, which is a corollary of the consensus nature of Japanese business decisions on operating problems—after all, if product design and manufacturing method decisions are made by a group on the lower levels of the organization, the pattern will be established for strategic and investment decisions to be made by a group on the upper levels. I think that we can also assume that Mr. Kotchian had been warned by his staff of the interlocking structure of Japanese business firms and governmental agencies. But no Westerner can be fully prepared for the intricate maneuvering which this combination of group decision making and interlocking organizational structures can generate.

These maneuvers, which Mr. Kotchian described as "Byzantine" in their complexity, extended over a period of 70 days. While he waited in a hotel room in downtown Tokyo, he was exposed to hurried meetings, intentional delays, midnight telephone calls and continual intimations that the decision was at hand. Being a foreigner, and acting as a salesman, Mr. Kotchian was excluded from the decision process. The agents retained by Lockheed could meet with the prime minister at his private home, for breakfast, but the president of Lockheed could meet only with the technical and functional representatives of the airlines, who might advise but could not decide upon the purchase. These meetings, delays, and telephone calls were played out against a backdrop of a declining order backlog and a deteriorating competitive position for the company. Lockheed had failed over the prior two years to obtain orders from Alitalia, Lufthansa, and Sabena in Europe, and a large foreign order was needed to bring unit sales above the break-even volume and re-pay the engineering expense. The agents for Lockheed calmly assumed that "pledges" would be made, and they explained that payments would be required to ensure the sale of twenty planes to Nippon, in Japan. Perhaps Mr. Kotchian wondered, as he sat in that hotel room waiting for the next meeting or the next tele-phone call, if other aircraft suppliers had made those pledges in Europe, for the TriStar was an acceptable design, certainly equal to the competition. Probably he worried about the future of his company; the loss of the Nippon order, for more than $430 mil-lion in total revenues, would mean the forfeiture of sales mo-mentum, the slowdown of design projects, and the discharge of production workers. He decided, and let us credit him with con-siderable worry and concern in that decision, to make the pledges and pay the bribes.

It is certainly easy for everyone now to condemn the decision by Mr. Kotchian to pay $3.8 million to government officials in Japan. It is much harder for most people to say that, faced with the same conditions of personal isolation, factual uncertainty, and corporate responsibility, they would not have reached the same decision. In this instance, the ethical dilemma is compli-cated by the presence of the mixed outcomes—political payoffs in Tokyo resulted in full employment in Burbank, California—and the career implications—Mr. Kotchian did not mention the possibility in his account, but it certainly has to be recognized that he would probably have been replaced as president had Lockheed lost the fourth foreign order in a row. If blame is to be ascribed—and it has to be in this instance, for here the brib-ery payments were blatant, dishonest and large—then members of the corporate staff should bear at least part of the responsi-bility, for they had failed to advise Mr. Kotchian of the likelihood of payoff demands so that other alternatives could have been considered in advance. It is hard to think of options when de-mands for very substantial amounts of money are presented in a matter-of-fact manner by high government officials, with the ob-vious endorsement and approval of the agents for your own firm.

I have tried to describe the bribe payment by Lockheed in a reasonably sympathetic light, giving some of the extenuating cir-cumstances, but—as I stated previously—I assume that most of us agree that that payment was wrong. Why do we feel that way? Let us work through the multiple forms of analysis and see if we can substantiate our feelings.

Economically, the order was large, at $430 million. We doubtless could compute the potential profit based upon published income and expense data for prior years, but that does not seem necessary; we recognize that the order would have resulted in a substantial profit. Legally, the bribe was not unlawful; this payment was one of those acts that led to the passage of the Foreign Corrupt Practices Act, but at the time Mr. Kotchian faced the decision, payments to foreign nationals were not contrary to U.S. law. In utilitarian terms—greatest good for the greatest number—we can partially excuse the payment: the benefits of employment in Burbank are very immediate and very obvious, while the damages to the democratic process in Japan are not as obvious and quite diffused. It is in universalistic terms—everyone faced with the same set of circumstances must act in the same way—that we find definite support for our intuitive beliefs. Could we ever propose a rule that every president of a large company, faced with the potential loss of a critical order, should offer to pay 0.8 percent of the face value of that order as a bribe? In terms of justice—each act must benefit in some way the least advantaged among us—we definitely benefit only the most wealthy citizens of Japan. In terms of liberty—each act must help others to select their own course of action—we definitely restrict the ability of Japanese citizens to choose freely for themselves. I think that this multiple form of analysis leads us to agree: The payment was "wrong."

ETHICAL ANALYSIS AND A JUSTIFIABLE BRIBERY CASE

Now, let us look at a bribe that I think most of us can say was "permissible" if not "right." This example may be apocryphal, but it is another story that, if not true, should be. I have been told that after the passage of the Foreign Corrupt Practices Act in 1977, the board of directors of a large engineering and construction firm, with worldwide operations, decided that they would not only obey the law, they would enforce it. They set a limit of $50 that could be paid for minor services received, such as customs clearance or vehicle registration, in countries where it was customary to make those payments and where the salaries of the officials were low enough to indicate a general knowledge and acceptance of those payments. Higher payments for services were forbidden, and all payments for contract approval or sales assistance were banned. To convey this message, a group of senior executives was selected to visit each of the construction sites and supply depots. These were older men, with extensive field experience, and they were known and respected by the area managers, site supervisors, and job foremen. At each site or depot, the personnel were assembled, and the executives stated clearly, "You will not pay bribes above the stated limit, and those only for services where it is both customary and known. If you do make payments, either directly or indirectly, for amounts above $50 you will be discharged, despite your length of service, with no corporate sympathy, no retirement benefits, and no severance pay. We are going to run this company the way it should be run, with high-quality work and absolute financial integrity. If that is not enough, and if we can't obtain engineering and construction contracts based upon that combination, we will close the company."

The message was heard, probably with mixed reactions but doubtless with complete clarity, by the personnel at all but a few of the overseas locations. These locations were not visited because the executives discontinued their mission prematurely. As they were returning from a remote site in the tropics, the pilot of the local airline taxied to the end of the runway, parked under the broiling sun, turned off the motors and air conditioning, and announced that he would take off after he had received a gift of $1,200 for his daughter's wedding. The money was paid, but the executives returned to New York, for they felt that they could no longer support an authoritative policy on corrupt practices which they had been unable to obey.

My opinion is that it is unfortunate that they did so, for this is the most justifiable instance of bribery I know. I assume that most of you would agree. Why do we feel this way, and how can we rationalize our beliefs? Economically, the impact of the payment upon the performance of the firm was minimal, so we can disregard that form of analysis. Legally, we will have to admit that the payment was unlawful, for this event occurred after the passage of the Foreign Corrupt Practices Act, but we saw in the chapter on the rule of law that legal requirements often do not represent moral standards, and that seems to me to be the case here. From the utilitarian point of view, I would think that the greatest good for the greatest number would come from the bribe payment, for otherwise the senior executives faced extreme discomfort and eventual illness in the stifling metal cabin of a grounded airplane, and the cost was minimal to others. From the universalist point of view, I should hope that we could agree that everyone condemned to this situation should be free to make the payment. The bribe does not decrease any opportunities for social cooperation, and it does increase the executives' ability to choose freely for themselves in the future, after release from the plane. I am not saying that I think that the extortion of the bribe by the aircraft pilot was in any way defensible, but I do believe that the payment of the bribe by the executives of the construction company was the "right" thing to do, given the situation.

ETHICAL ANALYSIS AND ETHICAL DILEMMAS

Multiple analysis is a useful means of rationalizing our intuitive beliefs, of justifying our almost automatic reactions, when looking at simple and obvious ethical issues, such as foreign bribery. Is it, however, a useful means of reaching a decision when we truly face an ethical dilemma, when the economic and the social performance of our organization truly do seem to conflict? Will it help us decide how much we owe to our employees, customers, suppliers, distributors, stockholders, and the general public? I think that it does, and here I should like to use as illustrations the ethical problems encountered by former students—the ones that were described in the first chapter, on the nature of ethics in management. I don't believe that in these examples it will be possible to assume agreement between us—we all have our own moral standards, based upon our different ethical systems of belief—so I will not state my conclusions, just my methods of analysis.

Pricing of Checking Account Services

Small checking accounts were determined to be unprofitable for the bank, and consequently it was felt that charges of $5.00 per month and $0.10 per transaction were warranted. The ethical problem was that the bank was in an urban area, with numerous older customers, many of them retired and living on Social Security, and the proposed charges would definitely diminish their standard of living.

How can this situation be analyzed? Let us start by considering alternatives. Is it possible to design a new type of checking account, perhaps limited to a set number of transactions per month, that would be less expensive to administer? Is it possible to completely automate the processing of transactions (checks and deposits) to further reduce the costs? Assuming that neither is possible, then let us move along to economic analysis. What are the costs of maintaining the small accounts used by older people? How much would those costs increase, if the bank were the only one in the area not to make a monthly or transaction charge to retired customers and consequently almost all of those people moved their accounts to this bank? What would the revenues be, if the charges were instituted? How many customers would close their accounts, even though they are naturally afraid to carry cash, and reduce both our income and our expenses?

Legal analysis is next. There is certainly no law against charging a fee for financial services, yet the bank can doubtless expect that some social and political organizations in the area would voice an objection to charging a fee that falls primarily on low-income, retired persons. The fee would contravene the presumed moral standards of a considerable segment of the population and might eventually lead to legal restrictions.

Last, let us think about moral analysis. Universalism—everyone faced with a given situation should be forced to take the same action or make the same decision—does not seem too relevant here; I would be willing to have every banker faced with unprofitable accounts charge a fee for those accounts, were it not for the unfortunate consequences of that action in this instance. Utilitarianism, which deals with the consequences, is relevant here; it is often translated as "the greatest good for the greatest number," but those two combined concepts don't really help in moral analysis because it is hard to measure the greatest good or identify the greatest number. It is more useful in analyzing ethical dilemmas to think of Utilitarianism as cost/benefit analysis, with the added step of considering who receives the benefits and who bears the costs. The benefits will go to the wealthier members of the community, as they are the large depositors who will receive the interest payments, or they are the stockholders of the bank who will receive the dividends, while the costs will be borne by the older and poorer people in the area. That is troublesome. It certainly goes against the dictum of Professor Rawls that inequality in the distribution of benefits is legitimate, provided it in some way helps the less advantaged members of society. It also goes against the dictum of Professor Nozick that actions should increase, not decrease, the ability of members of society to make their own decisions and lead their own lives.

How would I decide? I'm not certain—and I said earlier that I would not impose my views upon you—but at least I feel that I understand this situation much more fully and would be better able to explain my decision to others and support it rationally.

Exaggerated or Misleading Claims in Advertising

The ethical problem in this instance centered on advertising statements that were intended to deceive. "Up 387% over the past three years" was the heading on a mutual fund ad; it was accurate only over that specific time period—over a longer time span the fund had not kept pace with the growth in the Dow-Jones averages. "8½% interest" was the heading on a money market fund; there was a small asterisk, and down at the bottom of the page a footnote that explained that the interest rate was for the first month only. "Insured by [name of an insurance company]" was stated on every advertisement that mentioned customer accounts; the ads did not explain that the insurance company—which had an impressively fictitious name, such as Travelers Equitable of Wausau—was a wholly owned and poorly financed subsidiary.

How do we analyze this situation? Start once again by looking at alternatives; is it possible to develop an ad campaign that will be more effective and more truthful? I think we can assume that the client—a financial services firm—was not irrevocably committed to being untruthful; it just wanted an advertising program that increased its number of customers and believed that deceptive statements would accomplish that purpose.

If the client does not wish to change the approach, then it is necessary to look at the economics of the ad campaign. What is the probable increase in revenues that can be directly attributed to the deceptive advertising, and how do these marginal revenues compare to the media costs? Most of us would like to believe that misleading slogans are not effective; that potential customers quickly "see through" that sort of untruth. Perhaps, however, we will find from market research that the ads are effective. They clearly are not illegal—or we would not see so many that are similar in some sense—so we have to move to ethical analysis and moral reasoning.

Universalism seems to be most useful here, for the Utilitarian distribution of benefits and costs from deceptive advertising does not seem to be inherently unjust, and customers do have some obligation to be wary of untrue claims. The primary question of Universalism is, Are you willing to agree that every advertiser, wishing to increase revenues, should be free to make deliberately deceptive statements? Let me explain, once again, that in using this first formulation of the Categorical Imperative it is important not to think of the consequences of the act, for that would bring in Utilitarian concepts related to outcomes, and you would then not be building your ethical system of belief on a single principle. In this case, the single principle is your duty to other people to be consistent. You have to think about the type of world you want, and if you want a world in which judges don't try to deceive you, doctors don't try to deceive you, teachers don't try to deceive you, and friends don't try to deceive you, then you have to be consistent and agree that advertisers should not try to do so either.

You could also look at the second formulation of the Categorical Imperative: that it is necessary to treat other people as ends in themselves and not as means to our ends, which means that we should consider other people to be individuals worthy of dignity and respect, pursuing their own goals of happiness and self-improvement. The deliberate misleading of others does not seem to be treating them with dignity and respect; instead, it seems to be treating them solely as means to the goal of the deceptive advertiser.

Misuse of "Frequent Flyer" Discounts and Trips

Most frequent flyers travel on business. There is the ethical question of the propriety of giving the bonuses—which in essence are rebates on the price of the ticket—to the traveler and not to the company paying for the travel. The marketing reasons for doing so are clear: it is the traveler who decides which airline he or she will take. One can certainly look at this issue from an economic view; business travelers should be representing the owners of the company, and they are not exercising their responsibilities towards those owners in accepting the price rebates themselves instead of passing them along to the stockholders. The Utilitarian view is also relevant; the benefits go to the individual, while the costs are assigned to the company and to the nonbusiness travelers who normally do not fly frequently enough to accumulate enough discounts to qualify for a free trip. But neither view seems particularly compelling. Any company could insist that the rebates be returned to the firm, to reduce executive travel costs, and nonbusiness travelers are only being penalized because they don't travel enough to generate economies of scale in providing the service. Apparent inequities in the distribution of benefits or the allocation of costs that can be justified economically, legally, or morally are not truly inequitable.

The more interesting issue in this instance was not the ethical problem of the price rebates but the managerial actions of the executive who insisted that others in his department accumulate their credits for his use. This is not an ethical dilemma in the true sense of the term, for clearly there is no conflict between the economic performance and the social performance of the firm. This is an ethical problem only in that it represents personal dishonesty; it is theft, taking some property or benefit that belongs to others for an individual's own use. There may be no way the former student who explained this situation to me can prevent him from doing this to others—given that apparently the chairman of the firm either approved or would approve of the practice if he knew of it—but she can certainly prevent him from forcing her to participate. It would be very difficult for her superior to adversely affect her career for refusing to participate, for he could not accuse her of a lack of cooperation without accusing himself.

Working Conditions in a Manufacturing Plant

"The noise, the heat, the fumes and the pace of work are close to intolerable" was the statement made to me, yet it was explained that funds would not be allocated to improve conditions without showing a substantial internal rate of return. Here it would seem that economic analysis would be most meaningful. What are the costs in plant downtime, worker absence, and employee illness that result in low productivity and poor quality? How much could output and quality be improved, given better conditions? Economic theory insists that all costs be computed, including the personal costs of job safety and the social costs of environmental pollution; when this is done, remedial actions often do become economically rational.

Let us assume that this is an instance where improvements in the working conditions cannot be economically justified. Let us also assume that these conditions are marginally lawful. What do we do then? Obviously, we are forced to use moral analysis, but moral analysis looking at alternatives, not just condemning the existing situation. Utilitarianism seems useful here. Who receives the benefits and who bears the costs of closing the plant? If we reduce the work force or decrease the pay scale in order to make the improvements economically justifiable, then who receives what benefits and who bears what costs? It is difficult to conceive of viable alternatives in depressed basic industries such as steel stampings and iron foundries, but it is important in moral analysis to go beyond simple yes or no choices. Professor Rawls's concepts of social cooperation and distributive justice also seem relevant in looking at this situation: Which of these alternatives would most benefit the least advantaged among the members of the organization?

Customer Service and Declining Product Quality

The issue here was warranty repairs on new automobiles, and the hesitancy of both dealers and company representatives to authorize major work due to budget limitations. In the last illustration, we saw the necessity to look at multiple alternatives in ethical analysis; in this instance, there is a need to consider the extended consequences. The extended consequences of customer dissatisfaction with the product quality of American cars has been expressed as a growing market share for Japanese imports. That is not totally an accurate statement; other factors than a reputation for better product quality—among them lower wage rates and a favorable foreign exchange—have also been responsible for the trend towards foreign cars. But the economic results of such issues as poor product quality and adverse working conditions are a valid input in moral reasoning.

Extended consequences—the expected outcomes spread throughout society over the long term—are obviously important in ethical analysis. Some people have even claimed that an ethical approach to management is only the consideration of the long term rather than the short term and the recognition of the dispersed rather than the focused effects of a decision or action. This statement would appear to be an exaggeration, for it provides no means of analyzing those effects, but it does indicate the importance of looking beyond the immediate, concentrated outcomes.

Economic analysis would indicate generally a need for improved customer service in the automobile industry. Legal analysis would show certainly a widespread public insistence upon improved service, leading to the passage of "lemon" laws in many states. Moral analysis through Utilitarianism would seem to add little understanding: the benefits accruing to the customer would be exactly balanced by the costs allocated to the company, and it is hard to think of new-car buyers as the "greatest number" deserving of any "greatest good" in our society. Universalism and the Categorical Imperative are much more useful in this instance. Would we be willing to have every manufacturer of a defective product, when faced with a demand for repair or replacement, delay or attempt halfway measures? Would we be willing, were it our car or other product, to suffer that delay or that partial repair? The answer here would seem to be clear.

Work Force Reductions

This is a difficult issue because it throws the economic returns and the social obligations of the company so directly in conflict. It is necessary to look at the alternatives, but many of these alternatives are weak. Early retirement has a nice "voluntary" sound, but it is alleged not to be truly voluntary in some instances, and outplacement may be just a synonym for "We'll help you write your resume." The true problem may be that, given the competitive nature of many basic industries, the number of alternatives for meaningful cost reduction is limited.

Economic analysis is useful here. Exactly what will be the financial consequences of a smaller organization? Obviously, the overhead will be reduced, but will contraction improve competitive capability—in product development, market expansion, customer service, quality control, and worker productivity? It is necessary for us to admit that some organizations have become so large, with so many layers of middle managers and so many groups of staff between the senior executives who can allocate resources and the operating personnel who can use them, that it is hard to improve competitive performance without middle-management cutbacks. But it is also necessary to admit that many work force reductions impede rather than improve product development, market expansion, and so forth.

Moral analysis in work force reductions has to focus on Utilitarianism: who receives the benefits and who bears the costs, and is there any acceptable way to lessen those costs, or to redistribute those benefits? Here, high managerial salaries seem to be relevant; would it be more equitable to spend more on the retraining and assistance of displaced workers and less on the salaries and bonuses of senior executives? This is an issue which will be faced by many persons concerned with an ethical approach to management as business conditions become more global and more competitive, and as managerial salaries and bonuses become much higher and less market driven.

Environmental Pollution

Pollution is a major problem faced by our society, with obvious consequences for individual health, recreational opportunities, and the quality of life for all. Why does improper disposal of chemical wastes continue? Probably it continues partially because of the uncertainty associated with improper disposal; it is hard for many people to realize that 5 gallons, or even 50 gallons, of a chemical used routinely in industry will be all that harmful when dumped in a landfill or a stream. And, in many instances they are correct: 5 gallons or even 50 gallons are not that harmful in themselves; it is the aggregate of many 5 and 50 gallon amounts over a lengthy period of time that becomes exceedingly harmful.

In the illustration cited in the first chapter, a former student found that industrial solvents and degreasing solutions were being poured down a storm drain. I understand that, unfortunately, this is a common method of disposal. Economic analysis would reveal that the cost of proper disposal is often very high, which leads towards improper disposal. Legal analysis would show that this improper disposal is generally unlawful, but the law is difficult to enforce because of the problems of tracing the sources of pollution, whether the materials are poured into a public sewer or dumped on a vacant lot. The conclusions of moral analysis, however, would seem to be very definite. The greatest good for the greatest number obviously would indicate the need for proper combustion or burial, and few people would agree that all other firms, needing to dispose of used chemical compounds, should be free to just dump the material, secretly, into sewers or onto the landscape.

Property Tax Reductions

A major employer within a local community has substantial economic power, particularly if the employer has multiple plants in other locations and consequently can move production, and employment, between the plants. This economic power is often used in pressing for tax concessions. In the illustration given in the first chapter, a company was pressing for a 76 percent tax reduction, two years after it had received a 24 percent reduction. A large reduction of this nature would obviously impose tax increases or service reductions on the residents of the community.

Economic analysis would attempt to balance the benefits received by the community from the manufacturing plant, in the form of employment and tax payments, with the costs imposed on the community for the services needed by the plant and by the employees. But the balance of benefits and costs is not truly relevant in this instance. Here, we have to be concerned with the equitable receipt of those benefits and equitable allocation of those costs, and this requires the Utilitarian form of moral analysis. If we can establish, through legal analysis, that the tax-assessment procedures were properly followed by the community, and that the tax rates are approximately equal for all classes or types of property, then the question we face is whether it is "proper" or "right" or "just" for residents who are not employed by the plant, and consequently receive none of the benefits, to be forced to pay part of the costs. I promised not to state my opinions on these ethical issues, but in this instance I will break that promise: The use of economic power to impose economic penalties on others seems to me to be totally wrong.

ETHICAL ANALYSIS AND "DRAWING THE LINE"

Ethical decisions of the nature that have been described are not simple choices between right and wrong; they are complex judgments on the balance between the economic performance and the social performance of the organization. In all the nine instances that were discussed—except for the personal dishonesty in the instance of the airline ticket rebates—the economic performance of the firm measured by sales revenues, variable costs, fixed expenses, or net profits, would be improved. In all of the nine cases that were discussed the social performance of the firm, much more difficult to measure but expressed as some form of obligation to the managers, workers, customers, suppliers, distributors, and members of the local community, would be reduced. The question in each case became, in summary, What do we owe to our managers, our workers, our customers, our suppliers, our distributors and our community? How do we balance economic performance and social performance?

These are difficult questions to answer. They are difficult because of the essential conflict between the two dissimilar quantities: economic performance and social performance. They are also difficult because each question has numerous alternative solutions—these are not simple yes or no choices—and the consequences of the alternatives extend throughout society, with outcomes in which the social benefits and costs are mixed with economic benefits and costs, and the probabilities of those outcomes are frequently uncertain. How do we decide when faced with ethical problems of this complexity? Multiple analysis—using economic, legal, and moral forms of reasoning—appears to me to make the issues much clearer, and the "right" or "proper" or "just" decision more readily apparent.

Unfortunately, reaching the "right" or "proper" or "just" answer often is not enough. It is also necessary to decide when you will insist that your view of what is "right" and "proper" and "just" be recognized and then implemented by the organization. It is possible to explain your reasoning to people and gain some converts. It is possible to demonstrate your analysis to others and gain some more. But it is seldom possible to achieve unanimity in an ethical dilemma, because each individual's moral standards are so personal and so deeply held. Managers will often compromise on marketing and production and financial problems; they often will not compromise on major ethical issues.

What do you do when you feel strongly about an ethical problem—a conflict between the economic performance and the social performance of your firm—and you find that no compromise is possible? Do you walk away from the problem, or do you take some action? Where do you draw the line?

First, it is necessary to recognize that people can legitimately differ in their views of what should be done to resolve an ethical dilemma. A refusal to compromise does not automatically mean that others in the organization are wrong. People can differ on ethical issues because the relative weighting they place on the economic, legal, and moral forms of analysis may vary. People may differ because the ethical systems upon which their standards for moral reasoning are based can vary. And it is also necessary to recognize that people can differ in their views of what constitutes an ethical dilemma. Some people are much less concerned with social performance, and much more concerned with economic performance, than others. What do you do if you find a situation or an issue you believe to be deeply wrong according to your personal moral standards, yet you recognize that you are in the minority within your portion of the organization?

Let us assume that you are not the president or a senior executive of your company, able to take whatever action you believe to be just. Let us also assume that the firm has no ombudsman—generally an older and respected member of the organization who has been relieved of direct responsibility for management and designated to counsel privately with other employees on personal problems and ethical issues. Let us lastly assume that you have looked for alternatives and found none, and that you have tried to explain your concerns to your immediate superior and been rejected. What do you do? What do you do if you have found large amounts of toxic wastes being stored in leaking 55 gallon drums and been told, "Forget it; it's none of your business"? What do you do if you have found that employees are being subjected to unsafe working conditions and have been told, "We don't have the money to fix it"? What do you do if you find that payments are being made to some purchasing agents, to influence their decisions, and have been told, "Keep quiet about this; it goes on all the time"? Where do you draw the line, between what you will accept and what you will not accept?

This is the most fundamental moral issue in management, for it places a person's career in jeopardy. How do you decide if the resolution of the ethical dilemma you have encountered is worth your career? I think that it is necessary to use only the most basic moral reasoning:

Beneficiency. Who is going to be hurt, and how badly?
Consistency. Could I permit everyone to take this same action?

Justice. Will the least advantaged among us be treated the worst?

Liberty. Will this reduce our opportunities for free, informed choice?

In the next chapter we will look at changes in the structure and systems of an organization that can more readily resolve the ethical conflicts between economic and social performance, and more easily avoid the necessity for an individual to make the fundamental moral choice between his or her career and his or her responsibility.

CASES

George Spaulding

George Spaulding was a 1975 graduate of the M.B.A. program at the University of Michigan. He had majored in organizational behavior since he was interested in the general areas of industrial relations and labor negotiation, and had interviewed over the winter term for jobs in the personnel departments of large manufacturing companies. However, 1975 was not a good year for placement, and it was particularly not a good year for placement in the personnel function; the national economy was near the bottom of the post–Vietnam War recession, and personnel always seems to be one of the first areas to be cut back during periods of economic constraint.

George Spaulding, however, had an undergraduate degree in industrial engineering, which gave him a good background in quantitative analysis and computer programming, so that he was offered a position in a consulting firm in New York City that specialized in the design of computer-based systems for the evaluation of employees of industrial companies, public utilities, financial institutions, governmental agencies, etc. The consulting firm had grown rapidly, and George was one of four new M.B.A.s who were hired that spring; he got a bit of a head start on the others, however, since the academic year at Michigan ends in mid-April, and George was able to start work on June 1, three or four weeks before the others came.

> Consulting firms are somewhat like public accountants. There is no training program or formal sequence of assignments. Instead, you are given a desk in a large room and are expected to be available when needed by the senior consultants or officers of the firm. The first few weeks are pretty dull, since everyone else is too busy to bring you up-to-date on their work, so you tend to get very short assignments, such as proofreading a report or library research on a company. But, after about two weeks one of the senior consultants, a tall person from Texas who still maintained a Southwestern accent and tan despite 10 years in New York City, came by and said, "I have a big project down in Georgia, and you're going to have to do." That was not a very nice introduction to professional consulting, but it was just his style. (Statement of George Spaulding)

The senior consultant, whose name was "Tex" Harris, and George Spaulding spent the next two weeks in Georgia and Alabama putting together a proposal to design an employee evaluation and compensation/motivation system of a big electrical utility holding company in the South. They met with company officials in Atlanta to discuss requirements and potential problems in the system, and then visited division offices and field locations to talk to people there. The two men returned to New York to finish and submit the proposal, which was accepted very promptly. George was asked to return to the South to get further information about the payroll system and database structure, which differed for each of the operating divisions in the company.

> I spent four more weeks in Georgia, Florida, and Alabama, getting the data we needed to interface our system with the existing corporate records. I came back on weekends to see my wife, and to report to Tex, who always seemed pleased with my work, although he never said much that was complimentary. (Statement of George Spaulding)

George Spaulding finished the preliminary field work in the South on July 14 and returned to New York to help in the design of the system. He found that during his absence, two of the new M.B.A.s had been assigned to the public utility project, together with another junior consultant who had been with the company for two to three years. One of the first problems faced by the group was the need for additional programming assistance, since the size of the utility project easily outstripped the firm's own resources.

The five of us—Tex, myself and the three new people—had a meeting to discuss our requirements, which were fairly standard: a good knowledge of COBOL, and some familiarity with IMS and CFMS, which are integrated database structures. We talked about this, and I found that I knew a lot more about the programming requirements than did any of the others, partially because of my work at Michigan, partially because of my work in the South, but primarily because I had spent the last six weeks reading every book I could find on file design and database-management techniques. So, we agreed that I would interview most of the candidates. Then, just before we broke up, Tex said, "Look, let's agree that we don't want any women or blacks."

I was more surprised than shocked; it was so goddamn blatant. But, I didn't want to make a big issue about this, so I just told him, "That's illegal in New York City, Tex." He told me that it was perfectly legal to pick the people we wanted. I told him that it was against corporate policy, and he did get upset then, and told me that he would take care of the corporate policy and I could take care of the interviewing. Then, he calmed down and made some comment that I just wanted a woman to keep me company down in the South, and everybody laughed, and I thought that it had all been forgotten.

I did interview the candidates, and it was all so useless since we did not have a single woman or minority applicant for the jobs. But, you know what it was like to try to hire computer programmers and systems people on a part-time basis in 1975; the only people who were available were the hippies and the drifters. Some of them were damn competent, but they did not look like the typical occupants of Rockefeller Center; one of them who came in was barefoot, and many of them had hair down to their waists, or were wearing overalls. I picked the three best, but Tex did not like them, and he asked me, "Is that the best that you can do?"

Shortly afterwards, George went down to the South for another extended trip, which lasted three weeks. When he returned, he found that he had been removed from the public utility project, and reassigned to the pool of junior consultants in the outer office.

I talked to Tex, of course, but he told me that the utility project had been slowed down by the client, and that they just had to cut the overhead until it started up again full time. I sat around in the outer office for three months, doing meaningless little jobs for other people, sometimes even for the other M.B.A.s who had come in when I did. Finally, I saw the senior partner and told him about the lack of work. He told me that business had been slow that summer and that maybe I had better start looking about for something else. I will always be able to remember that conversation; it was the first time, and I hope the only time, that I have ever been fired. He told me, "We can keep you on for 30 days, or maybe even for 60 days, but I think that you ought to start looking seriously for something else."

I asked him, "How can you say you don't have enough work, when everybody in the office is busy, except me?" He became angry then, and told me, "We assigned you to work with Tex Harris, one of our most competent and respected people, who is good at bringing young men into the firm. Here is his evaluation report on you: Unsatisfactory attitude and uncooperative behavior. This is a small company, and we can't afford to keep people like that around. Now, I'm sorry, but I am busy this morning, even if you aren't."

I'm out, looking for another job, six months after I graduated from the M.B.A. program at the University of Michigan. And, I want to tell you, it is a lot harder finding a good position when you don't have a placement office to help you, and when you know that everyone you talk with will call your prior employer and get those very negative, and completely undeserved, comments. I don't know where I went wrong."

Exercise. What mistakes were made by George Spaulding?

Roger Worsham

Arnold Abramson and Company is a regional accounting firm, with offices in Michigan and northern Wisconsin. It was founded in 1934 to provide auditing and tax services in the Bay City, Saginaw, and Midland triangle in Michigan and, despite the depression, was immediately successful due to the economic growth of that area. Following the Second World War, the firm opened offices in Flint and Detroit, to the south, and in Traverse City, Petosky, and Alpena to the north. The northern offices were successful, and competition was very limited, so the company continued to expand across the Upper Peninsula, with new offices in Escanaba (1952), Marquette (1954), and Ironwood (1954) in Michigan, and in Rhinelander (1957), Ashland (1959), and Wausau (1961) Wisconsin.

The southern offices of Arnold Abramson and Company, in Flint and Detroit, competed directly with the large, national CPA firms, the so-called Big Eight, but they were able to operate successfully until the mid-1960s by providing more personalized services and by charging somewhat lower rates. However, competition sharply increased in the late 1960s and early 1970s as the tax laws became more complex, the auditing procedures more rigorous, and the bookkeeping more automated. The "Big Eight" firms were able, through their extensive training programs and their continual staff additions, to provide more extensive help and assistance to their clients on tax changes and data-processing procedures, and many of the small and medium-sized companies that had been customers of Arnold Abramson and Company for years switched to one of the national firms. It was eventually necessary to close the Detroit office and to reduce the size of the staff at Flint.

Some of the partners of Arnold Abramson and Company recommended the merger of their company with one of the national CPA firms, but the founder, Arnold Abramson, was not only still living but was still active, and he and his two sons were adamant in their opposition to any sale or merger. They believed that their past policies of personal attention, prompt response, and reduced billings would maintain the firm in the smaller cities and towns of northern Michigan and Wisconsin. Even when some of their clients in the northern areas of the two states felt it necessary to obtain the data-processing assistance and tax expertise of the national firms, Mr. Abramson and his two sons continued their resistance to the possibility of merger and continued to emphasize their concept of personalized service.

> The old gentleman was 84 when I joined the firm, and he simply was not going to surrender to Arthur Anderson or Price Waterhouse. And, you know, he had a point: There is room left in the world for the more personal approach, even in auditing. The old man was adamant about this. I understand that at the partners' dinner this year he laid it right on the line to the other members of the firm. "You are to keep the local banks, retail stores, and

manufacturers as your clients; if you lose your clients to those people from Detroit, we'll shut down your office." He always referred to representatives of the Big Eight firms as "those people from Detroit" even though they might be from offices in Lansing, Grand Rapids, or Milwaukee. (Statement of Roger Worsham)

Roger Worsham was a 32-year-old graduate of the M.B.A. program at the University of Michigan; he had majored in accounting, but he had found it difficult to obtain employment at the large national CPA firms. He had interviewed at eight of the largest companies and had been rejected by all eight. The director of placement at the School of Business Administration had explained that this was due to his age and that the Big Eight firms were exceedingly hesitant to hire anyone over 28 to 30 years of age since they felt that the older entrants were unlikely to stay with the firm over the first few years of auditing, which some people found to be dull and tedious. Roger Worsham, however, felt that perhaps his personality was more at fault than his age; he found it difficult to converse easily in the interviews, and he was afraid that he projected himself as a hesitant, uncertain individual. After graduating from college, he had worked for six years as a science teacher in a primary school, and interviewers always asked about his decision to change professions, seeming to imply that he was not certain about his objectives in life or his commitment to accounting.

At the suggestion of the faculty member who taught the small-business management course at the business school, Mr. Worsham applied to some of the smaller CPA firms in the state. He was accepted almost immediately by Arnold Abramson and Company.

> I met Mr. Abramson, Jr., and he talked about what I wanted to do in accounting, not what I had done in teaching, and that interview went really well, and I knew when he asked me if my wife and I would mind living in a small town that he was going to offer me a job. It does not pay as much as working for some of the other firms, but I can get my CPA (in Michigan, two years of auditing experience is required after passing the written examinations to obtain a CPA) and then I assume they'll pay me more, or I can move into industry. (Statement of Roger Worsham)

Roger Worsham was assigned to one of the northern offices, and he moved his family (wife and two small children) to the area and started work immediately after graduation. Within the first six months he participated in the audit of a savings and loan association, a farm equipment dealership, a large retail hardware store, and a nearly bankrupt machinery manufacturing firm. His family enjoyed the area in which they were living, he enjoyed the work that he was doing, and he felt that his life was beginning to take on a direction and purpose. But then he found clear evidence of fraud and encountered a situation that threatened his newly found security and employment.

> We were doing the annual audit for the machinery manufacturer. This company had not been doing well; sales had been declining for four or five years, losses had been reported for each of those years, and the financial position of the company had steadily deteriorated. I was going through the notes payable and found that they had a loan, and a large one, from the savings and loan association in [name of the city in which Mr. Worsham and his family lived].
>
> Now, firstly it is illegal for a savings and loan association to make a loan to a manufacturing firm; they are restricted by law to mortgages based upon residential real estate. But, even more, I knew this loan was not on the books of the savings and loan since I had been the one to audit the loan portfolio there. I had looked at every loan in the file—I had not statistically sampled from the file, which is the way you would usually do it—and had checked each loan to see that it was supported by a properly assigned mortgage and a currently valid appraisal. The only thing I had not done was to add up the total for the file to check with the reported total, since the usual way is to sample, and you don't get a total when you sample. I still had my working papers back at our office, of course, so I went back and ran the total and, sure enough, it was off by the amount of the loan to the manufacturing company.
>
> It was obvious what had happened: someone had taken the folder cover of the illegal loan out of the file prior to our audit. It became obvious who had done it: the president of the savings and loan association was a lawyer in the town who, I found by checking the stockholder lists, was the largest owner of the manufacturing company. He was also on the board of directors of the local bank and reputedly was a wealthy, powerful person in the community.
>
> I took my working papers and a Xerox copy of the ledger showing the loan and went to see the partner in charge of our office the next morning. He listened to me, without saying a word, and when I finished, he told me, "I will take care of this privately. We simply cannot afford to lose a client of the status of [name of the lawyer]. You put the papers you have through the shredder."

I was astonished. The AICPA code of ethics and the generally accepted auditing standards both require that you either resign from the engagement or issue an adverse opinion when you find irregularities. This was not a small amount. The loan was not only illegal, it was in default, and would adversely affect the savings and loan association.

I hesitated, because I was surprised and shocked, and he told me, "I will not tell you again. You put those papers through the shredder or I'll guarantee that you'll never get a CPA in Michigan, or work in an accounting office in this state for the rest of your life."

I didn't know what to do. (Statement of Roger Worsham)

Exercise. Make a specific recommendation to Roger Worsham regarding his future actions.

Susan Shapiro

Susan Shapiro was a 1970 graduate of Smith College, where she had majored in chemistry, and a 1971 graduate of M.I.T. with a Master of Science degree, also in chemistry, who came to the M.B.A. program at the University of Michigan after working for one year as a research chemist at Parke-Davis and Company in Ann Arbor.

One of the reasons I came back to get an M.B.A. was that the scientists at Parke-Davis, which is a large drug company with an advanced research division in Ann Arbor, simply weren't ready for women in the laboratory. It got to the stage that there was going to be an armed confrontation the next time some male told me to get his coffee or write up his experiment. Chemistry labs aren't great places for confrontations—there's so much expensive equipment around that can get broken—so I decided that I ought to get either a Ph.D. or an M.B.A. I chose the M.B.A. because it only took two years, and because most companies seemed to accept women more fully in an administrative role than in a technical capacity. (Statement of Susan Shapiro)

Susan graduated from Michigan in the lower half of her M.B.A. class. This was partially because she felt that some of her courses, such as marketing, were exploitive; partially because she refused to work or study on Saturdays due to religious convictions; but primarily because she returned to the second year of the M.B.A. program seven weeks late.

> I spent the summer of 1973 in Israel, working on a kibbutz in the north, near the Lebanon border. The Yom Kippur War started that fall. I don't think that a good Jew ought to leave Israel just because a war starts, so I stayed and worked as a volunteer in a military hospital until the need was past. Then I came back. Some of my professors understood, but most of them wanted me to make up the missed work, and there wasn't enough time in the rest of the term. I got three C's that term, and that really pulled my grade average down. (Statement of Susan Shapiro)

Susan enjoyed the quantitative aspects of finance and economics, and she interviewed with a number of firms for a position as a financial analyst. She found, however, that many of these companies evidently considered the grade point average strongly in their selection procedures for positions in corporate finance, and she received very few invitations for plant visits. Also, 1974 was a recession year, which of course reduced the employment opportunities for all the members of her class, but she felt that her job search was more difficult than that of many of her friends, and she thought that this was due to her low class standing.

> By 1974, companies had gotten over hiring women despite their sex and were beginning to hire women because of it. So I don't think being a woman hurt me. And I hope being a Jew didn't hurt me, but you never know. My grades were good, except for the third term, and for the marketing course. I explained the reason to all the interviewers, and they would nod their heads, but evidently they did not understand. Two of the interviewers asked if I planned to take vacations in Israel after I started working; what business is that of theirs? (Statement of Susan Shapiro)

Representatives of two large chemical companies came to Michigan near the end of the interview period; both of them were interested in Susan because of her undergraduate and graduate work in chemistry and her experience with Parke-Davis. Both companies invited her for plant visits; both extended job offers; and Susan accepted the offer from the company with corporate offices in New York City, close to her family and friends. She started the training program with that company in July, 1974.

We spent about three weeks in New York City, being told about the structure of the company and the uses of the products, and then they took us down to Baton Rouge, to look at a chemical plant. You realize that most of the M.B.A.s who go to work for a chemical company have very little knowledge of chemistry. There were 20 of us who started in the training program, and the others generally had undergraduate degrees in engineering or economics. I don't know what you learn by looking at a chemical plant, but they flew us down South, put us up at a Holiday Inn, and took us on a tour of their plant the next day. (Statement of Susan Shapiro)

During the plant tour, the management trainees were taken into a drying room where an intermediate chemical product was being washed with benzine and then dried. The cake was dumped in a rotating screen and sprayed with benzine, which was then partially recovered by a vacuum box under the screen. However, much of the solvent evaporated within the room, and the atmosphere was heavy with benzine fumes.

Benzine is a known carcinogen; there is a direct, statistically valid correlation between benzine and leukemia and birth defects. The federal standard is 10 parts per million, and a lab director would get upset if you let the concentration get near 100 parts for more than a few minutes, but in the drying room it was over 1,000. The air was humid with the vapor, and the eyes of the men who were working in the area were watering. I was glad to get out, and we were only in the drying room about five minutes.

I told the foreman who was showing us around—he was a big, burly man with probably 30 years' experience—that the conditions in the room were dangerous to the health of the men working there, but he told me, "Lady, don't worry about it. That is a sign-on job [a job to which newly hired employees are assigned until they build up their seniority so that they can transfer to more desirable work]; we've all done it, and it hasn't hurt any of us."

That night, back at the motel, I went up to the director of personnel, who was in charge of the training program, and told him about the situation. He was more polite than the foreman, but he said the same thing. "Susan, you can't change the company in the first month. Wait awhile; understand the problems, but don't be a troublemaker right at the start."

I don't want to lose this job, but I don't want to keep it at the expense of those men getting leukemia, or their children having birth defects. What should I do? (Statement of Susan Shapiro)

Exercise. Make a specific recommendation to Susan Shapiro regarding her future course of action.

CHAPTER **6**

Managerial Ethics and Organizational Design

I think that we can assume that the senior executives at most business firms want members of those firms to act in ways that they would consider to be "right" and "proper" and "just." I think that we can also be reasonably certain that the senior executives at most business firms want members of those firms to act in ways that will not offend a majority of the population and not receive adverse publicity from the nation's media, both newspapers and television. Yet, this happens repeatedly. Let us look at a few examples. General Electric Corporation, a firm with a reputation for excellence and one inevitably included on lists of the best-managed companies in the world, in 1985 was convicted on charges of defrauding the government.

> For years, General Electric Co. has been regarded as one of the nation's exemplary companies, a tough but fair competitor, a breeding ground for managerial excellence, and a good corporate citizen.
> Along the way, it has also acquired a less enviable record. Three times in the past 25 years, GE has been convicted of crimes: price fixing, bribery and fraud. The latest came in April, when GE pleaded guilty to charges of defrauding the government on missile-warhead contracts. That defense-contract investigation continues, promising to yield still more embarrassing headlines for the company.
> GE wasn't the only company singled out for misconduct in any of these cases. But its carefully burnished public persona made

151

GE's crimes particularly jarring. That they occurred at all—and how the company's top management responded—suggest how easily ethical standards can become blurred within big organizations.[1]

General Dynamics was another defense contractor that was accused of defrauding the government through improper billings and inaccurate cost allocations:

> On April 5, the Pentagon froze all contract payments, amounting to scores of millions of dollars per month, to General Dynamics as part of an effort to recoup $244 million in billings determined by the Defense Contract Audit Agency to be improper. In testimony before the House Energy and Commerce Committee's oversight subpanel on February 28, Mr. Lewis, the company's chief executive, had conceded a wide range of unallowable billings for entertainment and lobbying costs.[2]

Defense contractors are not the only companies whose employees have taken actions that most of us would consider to be improper and then have had those actions reported extensively by the press. E. F. Hutton, one of the largest and most respected of the retail brokerage firms, pleaded guilty in the summer of 1985 to a check-overdraft scheme that allegedly defrauded approximately 400 smaller banks. The intentional overdrafts gave Hutton the interest-free use of up to $250 million, and the scheme is said to have cost the banks as much as $8 million.

> When trading in E. F. Hutton & Co.'s stock was halted early on May 2, New York Stock Exchange traders assumed that a buyout of the widely respected brokerage giant was imminent. Instead, over the ticker came the shocking news that Hutton was pleading guilty to 2,000 separate counts of mail and wire fraud. . . . "We were very surprised," says a veteran executive at a rival firm. "The Street generally viewed Hutton like Caesar's wife—beyond suspicion."[3]

Not all of these decisions and actions that seem unethical to many of us involved millions of dollars. Some were for quite small amounts of money.

> It was a month before Christmas 1983, and Katherine Snow, an unmarried mother, needed money. Subsisting on a monthly income of only $423, Ms. Snow sought help from Thorp Finance Corp., Wisconsin's biggest consumer-loan company.
> Thorp, a unit of ITT Corp., the New York based conglomerate, agreed to lend Ms. Snow $126.72. But it also induced Ms. Snow to

borrow $14.72 for credit life insurance, $73.44 for property insurance and $202 for term life insurance. Finally, for an additional $24.50, Ms. Snow became a member of the ITT Consumer Thrift Club, entitling her to discounts on consumer products.

. . . Ms. Snow was a victim of "packing," a lucrative practice in which a lender adds payments for "optional" insurance and other products to the amount of the loan without the customer's requesting them.[4]

All these actions were, it was stated later in the articles from which I have quoted, directly contrary to the policies of the companies involved. Yet, they occurred. The purpose of this chapter is to consider why they occurred, and what can be done to prevent their reoccurrence. Let us consider prevention first, for there are two widely known means—ethical codes and ombudsman positions—and we want to evaluate their effectiveness. If either or both truly are effective at ensuring that the moral standards of the senior executives are known and followed throughout the organization, then the events described above were just anomalies, and we don't have to worry about the causes. If ethical codes and ombudsmen are not effective, then we do have to examine the causes of unethical actions in organizations and correct or eliminate those causes.

ETHICAL CODES

Ethical codes are statements of the norms and beliefs of an organization. These norms and beliefs are generally proposed, discussed, and defined by the senior executives in the firm and then published and distributed to all of the members. Norms, of course, are standards of behavior; they are the ways the senior people in the organization want the others to act when confronted with a given situation. An example of a norm in a code of ethics would be, "Employees of this company will not accept personal gifts with a monetary value over $25 in total from any business friend or associate, and they are expected to pay their full share of the costs for meals or other entertainment (concerts, the theatre, sporting events, etc.) that have a value above $25 per person." The norms in an ethical code are generally expressed as a series of negative statements, for it is easier to list the things a person should not do than to be precise about the things a person should do.

The beliefs in an ethical code are standards of thought; they are the ways that the senior people in the organization want others to think. This is not censorship. Instead, the intent is to encourage ways of thinking and patterns of attitudes that will lead towards the wanted behavior. Consequently, the beliefs in an ethical code are generally expressed in a positive form. "Our first responsibility is to our customer" is an example of a positive belief that commonly appears in codes of ethics; another would be "We wish to be good citizens of every community in which we operate." Some company codes of ethics appears in Figures 6–1 and 6–2.

Do ethical codes work? Are they helpful in conveying to all employees the moral standards selected by the board of directors and president? Not really. The problem is that it is not possible to state the norms and beliefs of an organization relative to the various constituent groups—employees, customers, suppliers, distributors, stockholders, and the general public—clearly and explicitly, without offending at least one of those groups. It is not possible to say, for example, that a company considers its employees to be more important to the success of the firm than its stockholders, without putting the stockholders on notice that profits and dividends come second. Stockholders, and their agents at trust departments and mutual funds, tend to resent that, just as the employees would if the conditions were reversed. Consequently, codes of ethics are usually written in general terms, noting obligations to each of the groups but not stating which takes precedence in any given situation.

The basic difficulty with codes of ethics is that they do not establish priorities between the norms and beliefs. The priorities are the true values of a firm, and they are not included. As an example, let us say that one division in a firm is faced with declining sales and profits; the question is whether to reduce middle-management employment and cut overhead costs—the classic downsizing decision—but the code of ethics says in one section that we respect our employees and in another section that we expect "fair" profits. How do we decide? What is "fair" in this instance? The code of ethics does not tell us.

Let us look at two other examples very briefly. Another division in our company is in a market that has grown very rapidly and has now reached such a large size that direct distribution from the factory to the retail outlets would be much more economical. Our code of ethics says that we will "work closely with

FIGURE 6–1
The Ethics Code of Borg-Warner Corporation, "To Reach beyond the Minimal"

Any business is a member of a social system, entitled to the rights and bound by the responsibilities of that membership. Its freedom to pursue economic goals is constrained by law and channeled by the forces of a free market. But these demands are minimal, requiring only that a business provide wanted goods and services, compete fairly, and cause no obvious harm.

For some companies that is enough. It is not enough for Borg-Warner. We impose upon ourselves an obligation to reach beyond the minimal. We do so convinced that by making a larger contribution to the society that sustains us, we best assure not only its future vitality, but our own.

This is what we believe. . . .

We believe in the dignity of the individual. However large and complex a business may be, its work is still done by people dealing with people. Each person involved is a unique human being, with pride, needs, values and innate personal worth. For Borg-Warner to succeed we must operate in a climate of openness and trust, in which each of us freely grants others the same respect, cooperation and decency we seek for ourselves.

We believe in our responsibility to the common good. Because Borg-Warner is both an economic and social force, our responsibilities to the public are large. The spur of competition and the sanctions of the law give strong guidance to our behavior, but alone do not inspire our best. For that we must heed the voice of our natural concern for others. Our challenge is to supply goods and services that are of superior value to those who use them; to create jobs that provide meaning for those who do them; to honor and enhance human life, and to offer our talents and our wealth to help improve the world we share.

We believe in the endless quest for excellence. Though we may be better today than we were yesterday, we are not as good as we must become. Borg-Warner chooses to be a leader—in serving our customers, advancing our technologies, and rewarding all who invest in us their time, money, and trust. None of us can settle for doing less than our best, and we can never stop trying to surpass what already have been achieved.

We believe in continuous renewal. A corporation endures and prospers only by moving forward. The past has given us the present to build on. But to follow our visions to the future, we must see the difference between traditions that give us continuity and strength, and conventions that no longer serve us—and have the course to act on that knowledge. Most can adapt after change has occurred; we must be among the few who anticipate change, shape it to our purpose, and act as its agents.

We believe in the commonwealth of Borg-Warner and its people. Borg-Warner is both a federation of businesses and a community of people. Our goal is to preserve the freedom each of us needs to find personal satisfaction while building the strength that comes from unity. True unity is more than a melding of self-interests; it results when values and ideals are also shared. Some of ours are spelled out in these statements of belief. Others include faith in our political, economic and spiritual heritage; pride in our work and our company; the knowledge that loyalty must flow in many directions; and a conviction that ownership is strongest when shared. We look to the unifying force of these beliefs as a source of energy to brighten the future of our company and all who depend on it.

SOURCE: Company booklet, published 1982.

FIGURE 6–2

The Ethics Code of Johnson and Johnson, "Our Credo"

We believe our first responsibility is to the doctors, nurses and patients, to mothers and all others who use our products and services.
In meeting their needs everything we do must be of high quality.
We must constantly strive to reduce our costs in order to maintain reasonable prices.
Customers' orders must be serviced promptly and accurately.
Our suppliers and distributors must have an opportunity to make a fair profit.

We are responsible to our employees, the men and women who work with us throughout the world.
Everyone must be considered as an individual.
We must respect their dignity and recognize their merit.
They must have a sense of security in their jobs.
Compensation must be fair and adequate, and working conditions clean, orderly and safe.
Employees must feel free to make suggestions and complaints.
There must be equal opportunity for employment, development and advancement for those qualified.
We must provide competent management, and their actions must be just and ethical.

We are responsible to the communities in which we live and work and to the world community as well.
We must be good citizens—support good works and charities and bear our fair share of taxes.
We must encourage civic improvements and better health and education.
We must maintain in good order the property we are privileged to use, protecting the environment and natural resources.

Our final responsibility is to our stockholders.
Business must make a sound profit.
We must experiment with new ideas.
Research must be carried on, innovative programs developed and mistakes paid for.
New equipment must be purchased, new facilities provided and new products launched.
Reserves must be created to provide for adverse times.
When we operate according to these principles, the stockholders should realize a fair return.

SOURCE: Company annual report for 1982, p. 5.

our suppliers and distributors, for they too deserve a profit," but perhaps we can reduce our prices to our customers, and gain a competitive advantage for ourselves, if we eliminate the wholesalers and ship directly. The code does not tell us how to choose between our distributors, our customers, and ourselves.

As a last example, we are fortunate in having within our company another division that also is growing rapidly; it needs to build a new manufacturing plant, but a town in an adjoining state has offered much more substantial tax concessions than the town in which we have operated for 60 years, and in which, let us assume, there is substantial unemployment and need for additional tax revenues. Our code of ethics says that we will be "good citizens" in every community in which we operate, but it does not explain how to choose between communities, or what being a "good citizen" really means.

Ethical dilemmas are conflicts between economic performance and social performance, with the social performance being expressed as obligations to employees, customers, suppliers, distributors, and the general public. Ethical codes can express a general sense of the obligation members of senior management feel towards those groups, but the codes cannot help a middle- or lower-level manager choose between the groups, or between economic and social performance. Should we reduce employment and increase our profits? Should we eliminate our wholesalers and cut our prices? Should we build in another city and reduce our taxes? Should we—and this is the reason I have included the code of ethics of Johnson and Johnson, Inc.—spend over $100 million removing Tylenol from the shelves of every store in the country after the nonprescription drug was found to have been deliberately poisoned in the Chicago area during 1982, causing the deaths of four individuals. James Burke, chairman of Johnson and Johnson, credits that code with guiding the actions of his company. "This document (the code of ethics) spells out our responsibilities to all our constituencies: consumers, employees, community, and stockholders. It served to guide all of us during the crisis, when hard decisions had to be made in what were often excruciatingly brief periods of time. All of our employees worldwide were able to watch the process of the Tylenol withdrawal and subsequent reintroduction in tamper-resistant packaging, confident of the way in which the decisions would be made. There was a great sense of shared pride in the knowledge that the Credo was being tested . . . and it worked!"[5] I think that we can agree that the employees of Johnson and Johnson should be proud of the response of their firm, which put consumer safety ahead of company profits, but we also have to agree that that response, and that priority ranking, is not unequivocally indicated in the Credo of the company.

OMBUDSMAN POSITION

An ombudsman is a person within an organization, often an older and respected manager, close to retirement, who has been relieved of operating responsibilities and assigned the task of counseling younger employees on career problems, organizational difficulties, and ethical issues. The term is Swedish; it refers to a government agent in that country who has been especially appointed to investigate complaints made by individual citizens against public officials for abuses of power or unfeeling/uncaring acts. Often the ombudsman can go considerably beyond counseling and investigation and is able to act informally to resolve problems. As an example, we can consider the case of the manager mentioned in the first chapter who is attempting to force all the employees working for him to use his frequent flyer card while traveling on company business. Were there an ombudsman in that company, the recent graduate of a business school who reported the practice to me could have reported it to the ombudsman. That person could then have counseled the recent graduate to "Forget it; lots of people do that around here," or he could have told her, "You do not need to be concerned any longer; I will take care of the matter and see that this is stopped, without implicating you in any way." Then, he could have met informally with the manager responsible and told him that the practice was totally unacceptable. An older and respected member of the firm, close to retirement yet also close to the president and members of the board, can correct many improper situations informally, without concern for later retribution.

Does the position of ombudsman work? Again, not really. The problem is that the person reporting the incident is not truly "not implicated in any way." We can assume that ombudsmen are generally discrete in talking with an offender, but the source of information for the ombudsman—the originator of the complaint—is usually awkwardly clear. It has to be a person within the organization who has a source of information about the practice and the moral scruples to report it. It generally is someone who has spoken to the guilty person about the practice within the past 30 days. It almost inevitably is someone who is easy to identify. The ombudsman does not have to be concerned about retribution; his or her contact generally does.

STRUCTURAL CAUSES OF UNETHICAL BEHAVIOR

We have seen that neither codes of conduct nor ombudsmen can ensure that the moral standards selected by the president and board of directors of a firm will be followed by all the members of that firm. Consequently, we will have to look at the causes of unethical behavior—the reasons why product managers at General Electric defrauded the government, and the reasons why regional managers at E. F. Hutton defrauded the banks, among other examples—and see if we can eliminate those causes. Let us accept the fact that at General Electric, General Dynamics, E. F. Hutton, and the Thorp Division of ITT, the individual manager who cheated the government, banks, customers, etc., did not directly benefit personally. These were not instances of managerial dishonesty. There were no payments, vacations, gifts. But the individuals did benefit *indirectly* from their actions. It is necessary to understand this indirect benefit, for this is the structural cause of unethical behavior within organizations.

Most large companies today are diversified, with numerous divisions. Each division normally consists of a given product line, a given market segment, and a given production process. Divisionalized structures of this type are generally decentralized: authority for product, market, and process changes is allocated to the divisional managers, who are then held responsible for economic performance.

There are two major problems with the divisionalized, decentralized type of organizational structure.[6] First, interrelationships between the divisions—in products, markets, processes, or technologies—cannot be utilized as the basis for economies of scale or economies of scope due to the separate nature of the divisions. For example, three divisions in one company, all using fractional horsepower motors in their product designs, or all using industrial wholesalers for their distribution channels, have no incentives in a decentralized structure to combine their activities. Second, corporate management in the decentralized structure has little control over the strategies of the divisions until after an outstanding success or an absolute failure has occurred; they are reduced to an ineffective review function. These problems brought changes in the management of diversification, starting in about 1975.

THE GENERAL ELECTRIC PLANNING SYSTEM

The General Electric Company led in the development of new methods for the management of diversity. GE, of course, is almost the archtype of a diversified firm, with numerous products, multiple markets, and different processes, and in the early 1970s it was organized in a decentralized structure, with approximately 250 product divisions grouped by industry type and evaluated by financial performance. Corporate executives, however, were said to be concerned that, despite substantial sales increases and continual technical developments, profits remained almost constant in absolute terms, and actually declined as a return on invested capital. Corporate-level executives were also said to be dismayed by their apparent inability to influence the strategy of the product division competing in the mainframe computer market, which eventually resulted in a write-off of nearly $300 million in developmental expenses and facility investments. It was felt that a new method of strategic planning was needed, to combine related divisions and to control divisional strategies.

The strategic planning method developed by General Electric was termed a portfolio model since it evaluated each product-market-process unit in the company as an investment that could be increased, maintained, or decreased over time, similar to the portfolio or assortment of investments in stocks and bonds held by a mutual fund. The product-market-process units at General Electric were termed "strategic business units," or "SBUs"; they consisted of a group of related product divisions that together had an ability to compete in an industry through a clearly defined strategy. Corporate management could then control that competition and direct that strategy through resource allocations by means of a corporate planning model rather than a capital budgeting process. The 250 decentralized product divisions at General Electric became 73 semicentralized strategic business units.

The underlying concept of the semicentralized corporate planning model developed by General Electric was the belief that each strategic business unit differed on two basic dimensions: the attractiveness of the industry and the strength of the company within that industry. It was felt that each strategic business unit could be measured on those two dimensions and then compared. As a result of the comparison, corporate resources could be channeled to the divisions that combined industry attractiveness and company strengths, because these were felt to be the divisions with the greatest probability of competitive success.

The attractiveness of the industry was measured on a multiple factor scale that included such inputs as the overall size of the market, annual growth, historical profitability, and competitive intensity. See Figure 6–3 for a listing of the factors and an example of the measurement process. The factors were weighted (by percentage) and then the business unit was measured (on a comparative rather than absolute scale of 1 to 5) for each factor to obtain an approximate value that could be summarized and used to evaluate the competitive posture of the SBU.

The strength of the business unit within the industry was also measured on a multiple factor scale that included such elements as market share, share growth, product quality, and brand reputation. Again, these factors were weighted and the business unit measured along comparative scales to obtain a summary figure.

Owing to the subjective nature of the weights that were applied to each of the factors, and to the inexact method of measuring along comparative rather than absolute scales, the summary figures for the attractiveness of the industry and the strength of the company within that industry were not used directly to evaluate each business unit. That is, a strategic business unit that measured 3.45 by 3.90, as in the example in Figure 6–3, was not automatically considered to be "better," or more likely to receive funding for future growth, than one that measured 3.35 by 3.80, or even 3.45 by 3.00. Instead, all strategic business units were grouped along each dimension, with one-third above average, one-third average, and one-third below average, and then they were visually displayed on a simple nine-cell matrix, again illustrated in Figure 6–3.

Business units that were above average on one of the dimensions of the General Electric planning model, and at least average on the other dimension, were considered to be optimal candidates for corporate investment and accelerated growth. Business units that were below average on one of the dimensions and no better than average on the other were felt to be prime candidates for disinvestment and eventual sale or liquidation. The balance of the business units were destined to be maintained at approximately the existing sales level and capital supply until either the industry's attractiveness or the company's strength

FIGURE 6–3
Factors, Weights and Measures for the General Electric Planning Matrix

	Weight	Measurement	Value
Overall Size	0.20	4.00	0.80
Annual Growth	0.20	5.00	1.00
Historical Margins	0.15	4.00	0.60
Competitive Intensity	0.15	2.00	0.30
Technological Requirements	0.15	3.00	0.45
Inflationary Vulnerability	0.05	3.00	0.15
Energy Requirements	0.05	2.00	0.10
Environmental Impact	0.05	1.00	0.05
Social/Political/Legal	Must be acceptable		—
	1.00		3.45

	Weight	Measurement	Value
Market Share	0.10	2.00	0.20
Share Growth	0.15	4.00	0.60
Product Quality	0.10	4.00	0.40
Brand Reputation	0.10	5.00	0.50
Distribution Network	0.05	3.00	0.15
Promotional Effectiveness	0.05	2.00	0.10
Productive Capacity	0.05	3.00	0.15
Productive Efficiency	0.05	2.00	0.10
Unit Costs	0.15	3.00	0.45
Material Supplies	0.05	5.00	0.25
R&D Performance	0.10	4.00	0.80
Managerial Personnel	0.05	4.00	0.20
	1.00		3.90

Company Strength within the Industry

Industry Attractiveness	Above Average	Average	Below Average
Above Average	Invest	Invest	Retain
Average	Invest	Retain	Divest
Below Average	Retain	Divest	Divest

SOURCE: LaRue Hosmer, *Strategic Management: Text and Cases on Business Policy* (Englewood Cliffs, N.J.: Prentice-Hall, 1982), pp. 311–12.

FIGURE 6–4
Market Share and Market Growth Relationships for the Boston
Consulting Group Planning Matrix

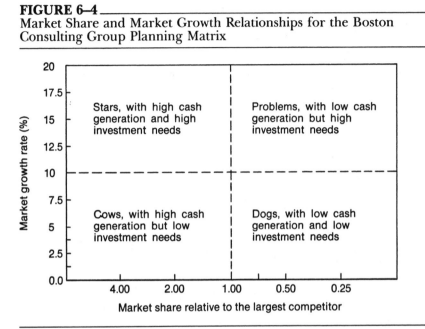

SOURCE: LaRue Hosmer, *Strategic Management: Text and Cases on Business Policy* (Englewood Cliffs, N.J.: Prentice-Hall, 1982), p. 312.

within that industry changed, leading then to increased investment and growth, or to gradual divestment and sale.

THE BOSTON CONSULTING GROUP PLANNING SYSTEM

The strategic planning model proposed by the Boston Consulting Group, though considerably better known due to "catchy" phrases and an active promotional campaign, is actually an offshoot of the one developed by the General Electric Company. The B.C.G. model—see Figure 6–4—avoids the problem of subjective weighting and comparative measures by assuming that a single statistic can serve as the surrogate for industry attractiveness, and that another single statistic can serve as the surrogate for the divisional strengths within the industry.

The Boston Consulting Group believes that the growth rate of the market, in percentage terms, can be used as a summary figure for the attractiveness of the industry, since high growth rates tend to be associated with high gross margins and low competitive pressures. High growth rates generally occur in the early stages of the product life cycle, before intensive competition affects industry prices, margins, and profits.

The Boston Consulting Group also believes that the share of the market, again expressed in percentage terms, can be used as a summary figure for the competitive position of the company within the industry because high market share tends to be associated with low production and distribution costs. The relationship between high market share and low competitive cost in the B.C.G. model is felt to be partially the result of the economies of scale that bring a constant decrease in average unit costs with each increase in annual production volume, but it is thought primarily to be the result of the experience curve that brings a continual decrease in average unit costs with each doubling of the cumulative production volume. The relationship between market share and market growth is generally portrayed in the B.C.G. model on a four-cell matrix, with the familiar "star," "cash cow," "problem child," and "dog" categories.

IMPACT OF PLANNING SYSTEMS ON MANAGERIAL BEHAVIOR

What do "star," "cash cow," "problem child," and "dog" categories, or for that matter, "above average," "average," and "below average" rankings have to do with unethical managerial behavior? They are determinant, given the objectives of the strategic planning models. Think for a minute of the possibility of your business unit being ranked below average on either industry attractiveness or company strength; what will happen to that unit? Lack of investment and a "wait and see" attitude on the part of corporate management are the best you can expect; disinvestment, and eventual sale or dissolution, are the most likely outcomes. What will happen if your business unit is positioned in the dog category? Your unit will be, if we continue to use the B.C.G. barnyard lexicon, "harvested," generally through sale of the unit or dissolution of the assets.

Is it propitious to a person's career to be "harvested?" There is little empirical data here, but there is substantial anecdotal evidence, all of which seems to indicate that the sale and subsequent merger of a business unit brings a degree of personal trauma, and the very real chance of dismissal in cost cutting efforts by the new owner.

Is it possible to avoid the "below average" rankings or the "cash cow" and "dog" categories? Yes, simply by increasing quarterly profits as a return on sales or as a return on the capital employed. In the General Electric planning matrix, profitability has a direct influence on the measurement of industry attractiveness through the input factors of historical margins and competitive intensity, accounting for 30 percent of the weightings. Profitability has an indirect influence on the measurement of company strengths through the input factors of product quality, brand reputation, promotional effectiveness and production efficiency, accounting for 35 percent of the weightings. The influence on company strengths is indirect because high profits are felt to be an indication, not a direct measure, of high product quality, good brand recognition, and so on.

In the B.C.G. planning matrix, high profits are assumed to be the result of high market share and high market growth. Consequently, the markets served by a given strategic business unit are segmented and redefined until the profit, growth, and share figures are consistent. This is not as unprofessional as it may seem; the need for consistency does force detailed examination of market segments and growth rates. For example, Mercedes-Benz has a very small share of the slow-growing total automobile market in the United States; a higher share of the more rapidly growing import automobile market; and the highest share of the most rapidly growing luxury automobile market both in the United States and worldwide. Mercedes-Benz profits doubtless reflect their secure position in that last market segment.

Can the managers within a strategic business unit alter the recorded profits of that unit, and consequently the position of that unit on the planning matrix? Yes, it is all too easy over the short term. In the noncompetitive defense industry, it is possible to change labor charges from a fixed-price to a negotiated-price portion of the contract, as was done by General Electric. Or, it is possible to switch wages from indirect to direct labor so that higher overhead rates may be allocated, as was done at McDonnell Douglas. Or, it is possible to simply add more overhead items, as was done at General Dynamics. Or, it is possible to lavishly entertain defense contracting officers—and perhaps contracting auditors as well—as was done by United Technologies.[7]

In competitive manufacturing and financial service industries, it is possible to improve recorded profits by altering product designs, by neglecting service warranties, by reducing repair-part inventories, and by changing the amount of capital allocated to the strategic business unit. Most companies now charge for both working capital and fixed capital, and those charges are a major expense item. By reducing the amount of capital recorded against a business unit, it is possible to improve both the numerator and the denominator of the return on investment ratio. In manufacturing, this leads to underinvestment in production processes and deteriorating working conditions. In financial services, where there is a credit for capital generated, this leads to the systematic overdrawing of checking accounts, as was done at E. F. Hutton. Prior students have told me that these financial manipulation practices are widespread. Automotive assembly divisions do not pay their small suppliers on time; this reduces the capital charged to the division. Commercial banks will arrange, as part of their regular services, to have customer checks drawn on distant branches; this increases the float. In what perhaps may be classified as the meanest of the capital-manipulation methods, I have been told that it is a common practice at the dividend disbursement department of a large bank never to respond to the first letter inquiring about the nonreceipt of a dividend check; older people may lose their checks, or move between summer and winter homes and the checks may not be forwarded. By refusing to respond to the first inquiry, the department receives a credit for those funds for 30 to 60 days, until the second inquiry arrives and is processed.

What can be done to remove these structural causes of unethical behavior, which can bring employees of an organization to act in ways directly contrary to the assumed moral standards of the senior officers? I think that we can assume that the president and members of the board of the large bank mentioned above would be infuriated at the practices of the dividend disbursement department, were they to learn of them. They will not learn of them because, under present conditions, it is to no one's benefit to tell them and it is to everyone's benefit not to tell them. Before going on to proposed solutions, however, let us look very briefly at another structural cause of unethical behavior: the control and motivation systems.

IMPACT OF CONTROL AND MOTIVATION SYSTEMS ON MANAGERIAL BEHAVIOR

Planning, control, and motivation are interrelated, both conceptually and pragmatically. Strategic planning looks at environmental assumptions, organizational resources, and managerial intentions and then settles upon a long-term strategy or method of competition within an industry. Program planning allocates the resources necessary to implement that strategy. Budgetary planning forecasts the revenues and expenses and establishes numerical measures of the achievement of the strategy. Operational accounting records the actual results of the achievement in numerical terms, and comparative evaluation analyzes the variances between the planned outcomes and the actual results. This comparison between planned outcomes and actual results is the basic control system or evaluation method, that is in use in nearly every major company worldwide. The control system or evaluation method is generally connected to the motivation system. Performance that meets or exceeds planned outcomes is rewarded, by acknowledgments—"you're doing a good job"—or by money—bonuses and commissions and salary increases—or by promotions. There is, in well-managed companies, a direct interrelationship between planning, control, and motivation; these interrelationships can be seen graphically in Figure 6–5.

People at all levels of an organization are interested in the acknowledgments, rewards, and promotions of the motivation system. The problem—and the second structural cause of unethical behavior within organizations—is that the actual outcome measures of personal performance can be manipulated just as can the strategic position measures of business performance. Design changes, inventory reductions, employee discharges, slow payments, process deterioration, workplace neglect, and environmental decay can all be used to improve personal performance measures, at the cost of other employees, and of customers, suppliers, distributors, and the general public.

SOLUTIONS TO THE STRUCTURAL CAUSES OF UNETHICAL BEHAVIOR

What can be done to remove the structural causes of unethical behavior in organizations? Unfortunately, less than we would

FIGURE 6–5

Relationship of Planning, Control, and Motivational Systems in Corporate Management

Planning System	Strategic planning (method of competition)	Environmental assumptions Organizational resources Managerial intentions Strategic alternatives
	Program planning (allocation of resources)	Net present value Internal rate of return Cost-benefit analysis Competitive position analysis
	Budgetary planning (projection of results)	Revenue forecasts Expense estimations Numerical measures Descriptive standards
Control System	Operational accounting (recording of performance)	Cost accumulation systems Cost allocation systems Responsibility centers Transfer prices and shared costs
	Comparative evaluation (analysis of variances)	Organizational control Program control Management control Operational control
Motivation System	Organizational response (design of incentives)	Perceptual response Financial response Positional response Personal response
	Individual response (actions and decisions)	Personal influence Interpersonal influence Social influence Cultural influence

SOURCE: LaRue Hosmer, *Strategic Management: Text and Cases on Business Policy* (Englewood Cliffs, N.J.: Prentice-Hall, 1982), p. 566.

like. We saw in the last chapter, on individual choice, that there are no completely satisfactory means of reaching a decision when confronted by an ethical dilemma. Multiple analysis—using economic, legal, and moral forms of reasoning—appears to make the issues clearer, and the "proper" or "right" or "just" decision more readily apparent, but the process does not guarantee unanimity. It does not guarantee unanimity because the values, the priorities between economic, legal, and moral outcomes, differ between members of every organization. In this chapter, we have to conclude that there are no completely satisfactory means of changing the planning, control, and motivational systems to guarantee that the moral standards of the senior executives will be followed. We can put less emphasis on the financial measures of performance—sales revenues, variable costs, fixed expenses, and quarterly profits—and more on the numerical measures— customer complaints, quality rejections, work force absences, community attitudes, and delays in responding to dividend inquiries—but these alone are not going to solve the problem.

The problem is that ethics in management represents a conflict between the economic and the social performance of an organization, and if that conflict is not specifically addressed and resolved by the senior executives within the firm, the natural tendency of the middle-level and operating-level managers will be to favor the economic side of the balance. Why? Because under current managerial systems, their performance is measured by economic criteria and their future is dependent upon economic results.

THE ETHICAL RESPONSIBILITIES
OF SENIOR MANAGEMENT

How can the conflict between economic and social performance be addressed and resolved by the senior executives within the firm? This has to be done as part of the strategic planning process. Ethical issues have to be made a part of that process, and no longer ignored or pushed down onto the operating levels. Hard ethical questions have to be asked by the managers in the business units, and specific ethical answers have to be supplied by the corporate executives. "We can substantially increase our revenues by charging $5 per month for all checking accounts below a minimum balance, but this will place a burden on many of our older, retired customers; should we make that charge?" "One of our major clients insists upon deliberately inaccurate statements in advertising; should we keep that client?" "We can reduce our costs by replacing the wholesale distributors who helped us in building the market; should we start direct factory-to-store shipments?"

The hard ethical questions have to be asked of the managers in the business units also. "What are the residues of this chemical process, and how are those waste materials being handled?" "What is the average delay in responding to an inquiry relative to a lost dividend check, and why does that delay exist?" "What are the working conditions within this plant, and how much would it cost to bring them to an acceptable level?" "What is the failure rate on this product, and are those failures being satisfactorily repaired?"

How are these hard ethical questions to be answered? My response is with character and courage. This is the character to face issues that have adverse social impacts associated with each of the alternatives, and the courage thoughtfully to evaluate each of these alternatives following economic, legal, and moral forms of reasoning, and then arrive at a decision. This is the character to recognize that personal costs may be associated with the choice, due to the biased nature of the planning, control, and motivation systems, and the courage to bear those costs.

Others may disagree with the final ethical decision, because of differences in their perspectives within the firm, or because of differences in their beliefs in the importance of economic outcomes, legal requirements, the moral principles of benevolence and consistency, and the moral values of justice and liberty. We have a multitude of economic, legal and ethical outcomes, requirements, principles, and values, but no clear ordering between them. This is not an excuse, however to avoid making ethical decisions in management. We have to make those decisions based upon our sense of responsibility to others; it is a test of our character and a measure of our courage.

Footnotes

1. *The Wall Street Journal,* July 5, 1985, p. 4.

2. *New York Times,* June 16, 1985, p. 26f.

3. *Business Week,* May 20, 1985, p. 110.

4. *The Wall Street Journal,* Feb. 26, 1985, p. 1.

5. Annual Report of Johnson and Johnson, 1982, p. 2.

6. For a more detailed discussion of strategic planning models, see L. T. Hosmer, *Strategic Management: Text and Cases on Business Policy* (Englewood Cliffs, N.J.: Prentice-Hall, 1982).

7. *Ann Arbor News,* June 28, 1985, p. F1.

CASES

Corrugated Containers and Antitrust Actions

The familiar corrugated shipping boxes that are used to package and protect both industrial and consumer goods are close to a commodity product. The liner board and corrugating medium used to make the boxes are manufactured by 26 different pulp and paper companies on very capital-intensive equipment. Originally the output materials were sold to independent box manufacturers, but in an effort to better control sales and better ensure the utilization of their expensive equipment, most pulp-and-paper companies have integrated forward and now manufacture their own boxes in small plants located near the major cities and commercial centers. It is difficult to differentiate corrugated boxes on the basis of quality, and most box plants have been designed to provide very prompt, often "same-day" service. Consequently, the basis of competition is price, and during periods of overcapacity in the industry, prices become very low, taking most of the margins.

The typical box plant is run as a profit center. The liner board for the outer surfaces of the completed box, and the corrugating medium for the inner reinforcing ridges between those surfaces, are shipped in large rolls at a transfer price that goes down with increased orders from the mill. The costs of both liner board and corrugating medium decline with volume because of the capital-intensive nature of the equipment that is used to produce them at the pulp-and-paper mill, and because of the highly skilled nature of the work force that is needed to operate that equipment. Pulp-and-paper-mill workers are seldom laid off because of the cost of retraining and replacing them. Consequently, with both capital and labor costs fixed, costs per roll of the liner board and corrugating medium go down rapidly as daily output goes up.

Labor costs at the box plants are generally low, as a percent of sales, because the process of making the shipping containers has been almost totally automated. The box-making equipment is high speed and technically complex, so the few workers needed tend to be skilled mechanics capable of both setting up and repairing the machinery. Again, with both capital and labor costs fixed, costs per completed shipping container go down rapidly as daily output goes up.

The manager of a box plant, the sales people, and the production workers strive to keep daily output as high as possible, for they are all paid a bonus based upon profits. Profits, and the resultant bonuses, can be substantial if sales prices are "reasonable" and if production volume is kept high, for all of the costs at the box plant decline with volume. There is continual temptation for the plant managers, and the sales representatives, to make agreements with their competitors as to ensure that sales prices remain at a "reasonable" level.

> The sales people get to know each other. They call on the same customers. They stay in the same motels. They eat at the same restaurants. It is very easy for one of them to say, "I'll let you take the business at X, if you'll let me handle the business at Y." It is also very easy for one plant manager to call another, and say, "You can have the contract from Z this quarter, but I want it next quarter." It happens all the time. Or, it did happen all the time until 1976. (Statement of industry analyst)

In 1976, 23 paper companies were indicted for price fixing in the sales of corrugated boxes. The government alleged that these defendants participated in a conspiracy from 1960 onward to allocate customers and to fix prices, in violation of the Sherman Antitrust Act. Twenty-two of the firms eventually pleaded no contest to the price-fixing and bid-rigging charges. A plea of no contest is usually considered to be equivalent to an admission of guilt, but that admission cannot then be used in any subsequent civil action, in which some of the allocated customers might sue to recover damages.

The judge fined each of the 22 paper companies $50,000. This was considered to be low, given the extensive nature of the charged conspiracy. The judge also suspended jail sentences on the plant managers and sales people who were said to have participated in the price fixing. This was considered to be generous. But, the judge did impose an unusually strict provision in the final settlement. Each year, for the next 10 years, a senior officer from each of the 22 pulp and paper companies was required to appear before him, prepared to demonstrate that the company he represented was not violating any of the provisions of the Sherman Antitrust Act in the sales of corrugated boxes.

> I think that the judge was lenient in setting the fines and suspending the jail sentences because he felt that the plant managers and sales representatives were just, in essence, carrying out the intentions if not the orders of the senior executives, but the responsibility of those latter people could never be proven. Consequently, he set up this special provision so that if it happens again, guilt can be established at the upper levels of the corporation. And, if it happens again, I will just about guarantee that some of those senior executives will go to jail, for failing to prevent price-fixing practices at the lower levels of the organization. If I were one of those senior people, I would be worried. (Statement of industry consultant)

Exercise. Assume that you are the comptroller of one of the pulp and paper companies. Further, assume that you have been instructed by the president of your company to appear before the judge each year and assure that person that the company is not violating any of the provisions of the Sherman Antitrust Act. Set up a system so that you will be able to show that price fixing is no longer practiced by the local box plants.

E. F. Hutton

E. F. Hutton is a large and respected investment banking and brokerage sales firm that, in 1985, had 413 branch and regional offices, 13,376 employees, $2,171 million in total revenues, and $110 million in aftertax profits. The firm also had, in 1985, a severely damaged reputation due to admissions by senior officers that, for years, the company had fraudulently obtained the use of more than $1 billion in interest-free funds by systematically overdrawing checking accounts at the company's 400 banks.

The process by which the excess funds were fraudulently obtained is known as *overdrafting*. It is complex, and requires concerted actions by many branch and regional office managers:

1. The manager at the branch office of the firm in, let us say, a northern suburb of Detroit might deposit $25,000 of customer checks at a local bank on a typical day. The manager would then draw a check on that bank for $50,000 (the rule that apparently was used by company employees was to double the daily deposits) and send that amount, hand carried, to the regional office in Detroit.

2. The manager at the regional office would deposit the $50,000 in a different bank, along with the "doubled" checks from other E. F. Hutton branch offices in the area, and promptly invest the funds in short-term securities, earning perhaps 8½ percent interest, for four or five days. At the end of that period, checks would be hand carried back to the branch offices, for deposit to cover the "over-drafted" checks when they were presented for collection.

3. The overdrafting process worked because checks deposited at a bank different from the one on which they are drawn are sent, by regular postal service, to a central clearing house operated by the Federal Reserve for processing. During processing, all checks deposited at a given bank are added to the daily balance of that bank's account. All checks drawn on a given bank are subtracted from the daily balance of that bank's account. Differences in the final balances between banks are then adjusted through credit transfers, and the checks are returned, again by regular postal service, to the banks on which they are drawn to be deducted from the individual customers' daily balances. E. F. Hutton benefited from the time differential between hand carrying checks rather than sending them by normal mail, which is a legal form of "cash management," but they doubled that benefit by creating fraudulent deposits.

The process was somewhat more complex than has been portrayed, in that branch managers within a given city, such as Detroit, would exchange checks drawn on different banks, to confuse the pattern of inadequate funds and sudden deposits. But, overall, it was charged that the E. F. Hutton regional offices made over $8.5 million in interest on nonexistent money.

E. F. Hutton pleaded guilty to the charge, after a Justice Department investigation that lasted nearly three years. By pleading guilty, the company avoided a lengthy public trial. But the episode certainly tarnished the reputation of the firm, which previously had been among the highest in the financial community.

> "We were very surprised," says a veteran executive at a rival firm. "The Street generally viewed Hutton like Caesar's wife—beyond suspicion."[1]

The damage to the reputation of the firm was particularly severe because many members of the financial community felt that the overdrafting practice must have been known, and tacitly approved, by senior executives at E. F. Hutton corporate headquarters in New York City. However, federal prosecutors agreed—in exchange for the guilty plea by the firm, the payment of $2 million fine, and an agreement to repay the $8.5 million in fraudulent interest to the banks—not to charge any individual member of management with participation in the crime.

Robert Foman, chairman of E. F. Hutton, acknowledged that the company had not installed controls adequate to prevent branch and regional offices from using cash-management and check-transfer methods that were "not consistent with either the policies or the standards of this firm" and said that the company would take "appropriate action" against employees who had participated in the scheme.[2] But, he added, senior management had halted the abuses as soon as they learned of them, and consequently should not be prosecuted.

Footnotes

1. *Business Week*, May 20, 1985, p. 110.
2. Both quotations are from *Business Week*, May 20, 1985, p. 111.

Exercises.

1. As a consultant employed by Robert Foman, chairman of E. F. Hutton, what recommendations would you make to ensure that overdrafting practices do not occur again?

2. Are there any other means of artificially increasing the profits reported by branch and regional offices in a brokerage sales firm, and what recommendations would you make to prevent those abuses?

General Electric Company

General Electric Company is a large and diversified manufacturer of electrical and electrically related products, with sales, in 1985, of $26.2 billion, and profits in that same year of $2.3 billion. The products of the company ranged from electric toasters to jet engines, in nine basic divisions that made the following contributions to the sales and profit totals:

	Sales	Profits
Consumer division: lighting equipment, video and audio sets, batteries, etc.	13%	10%
Appliance division: refrigerators, stoves, washers, dryers, dishwashers, etc.	12	10
Industrial division: semiconductors, electronic switchgear, motors and motor controls, etc.	14	3
Power division: generators, transformers and other equipment for the electrical utility industry	20	22
Aircraft division: jet engines for both military and commercial airplanes	13	12
Material division: plastics, silicones, and ceramics for high-technology applications	8	12
Technical division: a range of high-technology systems, for aerospace and medical use	16	11
Financial division: General Electric Credit Co., which provided leases and loans to industrial customers	2	15
Natural resource division: Utah Consolidated, a large coal-mining firm that was sold midway through 1985	2	5

There is no "Defense" division, though General Electric is one of the largest defense contractors, with over $4.7 billion in sales to the military. The industrial, aircraft, material, and technical divisions all work on contracts for both the Defense Department and NASA. This mixture of military, aerospace, industrial, and commercial work within those divisions creates an opportunity to transfer cost allocations from the industrial and commercial products, which normally are sold in competitive markets and have to be competitively priced, to the defense and aerospace contracts, which usually are performed on a "cost-plus" basis.

The opportunity to transfer costs from civilian to government jobs, and consequently to receive reimbursement for expenses that otherwise would have been charged against one of the divisions, was evidently too tempting to be avoided. The company pleaded guilty in May, 1985, to 108 charges that it had defrauded the government by altering time cards for hourly paid employees working on commercial products to transfer their wages to a Minuteman missile contract, and was fined $1,040,000. In two separate cases, the company agreed to pay $900,000 to the National Aeronautics and Space Administration to correct the misallocation of overhead costs to an aerospace product, and settled a $4 million claim with that agency for disputed labor charges. In a last instance, the Air Force charged that $168 million had been improperly expensed for work on aircraft engine parts during the period 1980 to 1984. The company strongly disputed this last charge and indicated it would seek a court trial before repaying any funds.

Charges of fraud and corruption are rare at General Electric, which has long had a reputation as one of the best-managed companies in the world. The company, however, under the leadership of a young and active chairman, has been undergoing substantial change since 1981. The chairman, John Welch, believes that international competition will intensify in the coming years, and he is said to be striving to make the firm more efficient and more entrepreneurial. In the last four years, $8.1 billion has been spent to modernize manufacturing and automate many production processes. At the same time, some of the older product lines have been sold, many of the obsolete manufacturing plants have been closed, and total employment has been reduced by approximately 18 percent. The corporate headquarters staff alone was slashed from over 700 people in 1981 to under 600 in 1984. There is, it is said, intense pressure on employees at all levels to perform, and to meet financial goals:

> "Is there pressure?" asks the 49-year-old Mr. Welch rhetorically, sitting in his spacious office overlooking the Connecticut countryside. . . . "Is it going to get tougher next year and the next and the next? The answer is yes."[1]

Footnote

1. *New York Times*, May 5, 1985, Business Section, p. 3.

Exercises.

1. As a consultant to John Welch, chairman of General Electric, what recommendations would you make to ensure that the fraudulent billings of the Defense Department and NASA do not occur again?

2. What other means exist of artificially increasing reported profits for a given product line or manufacturing plant over the short term, and what recommendations would you make to prevent those abuses?

Index

*This book has been set on the Mergenthaler 202,
in 11 and 10 point Baskerville, leaded 2 points.
Chapter numbers are 24 point Baskerville Bold
and chapter titles are 20 point Baskerville Bold
Italic. The overall type area is 27 by 47 picas.*